Ghosthunting
NEW JERSEY

AMERICA'S
HAUNTED ROAD TRIP

GHOSTHUNTING NEW JERSEY

L'AURA HLADIK

CLERISY PRESS

Published by Clerisy Press
Distributed by Publishers Group West
Printed in the United States of America
First edition, first printing

Library of Congress Cataloging-in-Publication Data

Hladik, L'Aura.
    Ghosthunting New Jersey / by L'Aura Hladik.—1st ed.
      p. cm.
    ISBN-13: 978-1-57860-326-8
    ISBN-10: 1-57860-326-9
    1. Ghosts—New Jersey. 2. Haunted places—New Jersey. I. Title.

    BF1472.U6H59 2008
    133.109749--dc22

                                    2008032884

Editor: John Kachuba
Cover design: Scott McGrew
Cover and interior photos provided by L'Aura Hladik

Clerisy Press
1700 Madison Road
Cincinnati, Ohio 45206
www.clerisypress.com

TABLE OF CONTENTS

long-lingering specters. From the ghost singing in the control booth to the "helper" ghost who hid the workman's hammer, Stanhope House is home to the blues with shades of "ecto-gray."

CENTRAL NEW JERSEY   133

in Kenilworth. Some claim that his spirit charges through the Watchung Reservation on horseback or appears near his grave in the Presbyterian Church cemetery in Westfield.

Once a royal governor's palace, now a museum and office space rental, the Proprietary House has the ghost of a little boy and a Revolutionary War soldier, and a very busy ladies' room.

Heavenly bodies of dancers aren't the only entertainment at this premiere gentlemen's club in South Plainfield, which may be the only haunted gentlemen's club in North America. The amorphous body circulating the parking lot begs for a closer look.

Known today for its fine dining and beautiful wedding receptions, the Cranbury Inn is still regarded as a major stagecoach stop by a man who died while falling off a coach there in 1796. The ghosts of a longtime female boarder and slaves on the Underground Railroad round out the cast.

SOUTHERN NEW JERSEY   221

Does the ghost of Joel Clough still haunt the prison's dungeon, where he was kept before being hanged for the murder of his mistress? Or is it just a residual haunting that continually replays?

Museum staff can tell you stories about more than just the artifacts on display. You'll hear about lights that come on by themselves, phantom footsteps and giggling, and a curiously musical wind-up doll.

Welcome to America's Haunted Road Trip

DO YOU BELIEVE IN GHOSTS?

If you're like 52 percent of Americans (according to a recent Harris Poll), you *do* believe that ghosts walk among us. Perhaps you've heard your name called in a dark and empty house. It could be that you have awoken to the sound of footsteps outside your bedroom door, only to find no one there. It is possible that you saw your grandmother sitting in her favorite rocker chair, the same grandmother who passed away several years before. Maybe you took a photo of a crumbling, deserted farmhouse and discovered strange mists and orbs in the photo, anomalies that were not visible to your naked eye.

If you have experienced similar paranormal events, then you know that ghosts exist. Even if you have not yet experienced these things, you're curious about the paranormal world, the spirit realm. If you weren't, you wouldn't be reading this latest book in the America's Haunted Road Trip series.

Over the last several years, I've investigated haunted locations across the country and with each new site, I found myself becoming more fascinated by ghosts. What are they? How do they manifest themselves? Why are they here? These are just a few of the questions I've been asking. No doubt, you've been asking the same questions.

You'll find some answers to those questions when you take America's Haunted Road Trip. We've gathered some of America's top ghost writers (pun intended) and researchers to explore their states' favorite haunts. Each location is open to the public so you can visit them yourself and try out your ghosthunting skills. In addition to telling you about their often hair-raising adventures, the writers include maps and travel directions to guide your own haunted road trip.

L'Aura Hladik's *Ghosthunting New Jersey* is a spine-tingling trip through the small towns and backwoods of the Garden State. Ride shotgun with ghosthunter L'Aura as she seeks the fiery ghost of Roxana at Mead Hall on the campus of Drew University and checks out the shadows and mysterious voices at the Whistling Swan Inn in Stanhope. And exactly who are the ghostly family captured on camera at the Publick House in Chester? Hang on tight; *Ghosthunting New Jersey* is a scary ride.

But once you've finished reading this book, don't unbuckle your seatbelt. There are still forty-nine states left for your haunted road trip! See you on the road!

John Kachuba
Editor, America's Haunted Road Trip

Ghosthunting
NEW JERSEY

AMERICA'S
HAUNTED ROAD TRIP

Introduction

TIMES SURE HAVE CHANGED. When I first started ghost hunting, in 1993, I booked dinners at restaurants reported to be haunted. I planned vacations at bed and breakfasts that offered paranormal activity in addition to a hot country breakfast. I found most of these places in two books by Arthur Meyers: *The Ghostly Register* and *The Ghostly Gazetteer*. I had to investigate under the guise of a birthday, anniversary dinner, or a romantic weekend getaway. I could not come out and admit I was ghost hunting for the real fear of being looked upon as someone destined to be fitted for a straightjacket.

A few years later, I acquired dial-up Internet access. Waiting for a Web site to open was the most exciting and anxiety-ridden way to spend ten minutes. Of course, the first thing I ever searched for was the word "ghosts." Up came a list of maybe three ghost-related Web sites. The site I visited, http://www.ghostweb.com, was hosting its first annual Ghost Conference. I thought, "Wow! Not only do these people post their ghost hunting on a medium for all the world to see, they're even gathering in person to discuss it."

The times changed further when I actually attended ghost conferences and decided to start a group myself, the New Jersey Ghost Hunters Society (NJGHS). The first meeting was at my home, and the place was packed. Literally, the overflow from the living room went out the front door onto the porch, up the staircase and down the hall and into the kitchen. The overall feedback I heard that day was, "I'm so glad you're doing this. It's great to finally meet other people who are into this like me." The meetings moved to the Community Center uptown and grew exponentially each month.

More changes came along in the form of digital photography. This caused a major rift in the ghost-hunting community, much like the debate on whether the Earth is round or flat. Digital cameras became smaller and more capable. My Nikon Coolpix digital camera is one fourth the size of my original Sony Mavica and takes pictures eight times larger.

Things really changed for ghost hunters when the Sci Fi Channel introduced its television show *Ghost Hunters*. This drove what we were doing right into everyone's living rooms. No longer would I have to hang my head in embarrassment and say, "I'm a ghost hunter." Now I could answer confidently, "Yes, like those guys on TV." In fact, more television shows came along on mainstream TV, such as *Supernatural, Ghost Whisperer,* and *Medium*. Ghost hunters are no longer relegated to reruns of *The X-Files*.

Thanks to this mainstream media and its resulting heightened awareness of the paranormal by the general public, I was able to come right out and ask the waitress at a restaurant situated in an old building, "So, do you have any ghosts here?" Without missing a beat or backing away while holding her fingers in the form of a cross, she answered, "Yes, the ghost of the guy who hanged himself here. The bartender has seen him and heard him walk down the stairs and slam the front door behind him, even though the door never moves—it's just the sound of it being slammed."

There are at least five cities in the United States claiming to be "the most haunted in America," each with its slew of ghost tours, ghost walks, and haunted B&Bs. Ghosts are not just for Halloween any more. But lost in the marketing and merchandising is the person who had a paranormal experience and wants to know "what made it tick." The true ghost hunter is all about the research and figuring out how and why something happened and whether it could happen again if the conditions were controlled.

Ghost hunting is thrilling, but it's also comforting. I've gotten calls from many families who were frightened by what they were experiencing and thinking they were losing their minds. Strange as it sounds, they're comforted when an investigation documents for them that a spirit or a residual haunting is taking place. There's been a lot of comfort experienced by those who joined the NJGHS. They were so happy to have a place to convene and discuss this interest openly.

So where should one ghost hunt first in New Jersey? That depends on the weather. If it's nice out, then visit the Spy House or Ringwood Manor. The Spy House has the bay breeze and a picnic area. Ringwood has its gorgeous grounds and gardens. If the weather is not cooperating, head inside to have dinner at Charlie Brown's Steakhouse in Hackettstown or tour Lambert Castle in Paterson. Guys can ghost hunt at Liquid Assets, a strip club in South Plainfield. Ah, the sacrifices men must make for the sake of research.

Reading this book will give you historical background and possible explanations for the haunting at each place. These are not the last word on New Jersey's ghosts and their places of inhabitance. It's a guide. You'll get an idea of what to look for, but the rest is up to you. Happy hunting!

Ghost Hunting 101

For those new to the research of ghosts and the paranormal, here is a list of terms used frequently throughout this book and the paranormal research community.

Orb or Orbs—These appear as balls of white light that can be translucent or opaque. Sometimes they appear to have a hue or color, either red or blue. In most cases, orbs are determined to be the result of the digital camera taking a picture of dust, pollen, or an insect. In most cases the orbs show up in pictures but were undetected by the photographer's eye.

Ectoplasmic Mist or Vapor—This anomaly is an amorphous cloudy or smoky appearance in photos. This mist shows up in photos even though the person taking the photo did not see any obstruction or interference when taking the photo.

Vortex (Vortices-pl.)—This anomaly appears as a tornado or funnel-shaped mist in photos.

Full Body Apparition—The ultimate capture for a paranormal investigator. Full body apparitions can appear as solid as you and I or as a shadow or pile of dust in the form of a human. They can be seen with the human eye as well as photographed.

EMF (Electromagnetic Field)—The device, an electromagnetic field strength meter, is used to track the EMFs during an investigation. It is theorized that a spirit or ghost will cause a fluctuation detected on the meter between 0.2 to 0.4 milligauss.

EVP (Electronic Voice Phenomena)—Typically the spirit or ghost's voice is not heard with the human ear, but is recorded with either digital or analog audio recorders. The movie *White Noise* dictated the accurate definition of EVP, but instead portrayed *ITC*—Instrumental Transcommunication. (ITC—voices of the spirit world are supposedly captured by having one's camcorder record the white noise displayed on one's television set.)

Residual Haunting—This is the effect of a traumatic or emotionally charged event leaving its mark in time so as to play itself over and over. Some residuals are audio only, some are video only, and some are both audio and video. Residual haunting is noninteractive with the living or the surroundings.

Northern New Jersey

Madison
Roxana: The Ghost of Mead Hall
The Ghost of Rose City

Totowa
Ladies in White

Paterson
Lambert's Castle

Stanhope
The Whistling Swan Inn
The Stanhope House
Bell's Mansion

Great Meadows
Shades of Death Road &
Ghost Lake

Hackettstown
You're a Good Ghost Charlie
Brown
Centenary College

Washington
Washington Theatre
The Changewater Murders

Newton
Yellow Frame Church

Ringwood
Ringwood Manor
Ho-Ho-Kus
The Hermitage

Chester
Publick House Restaurant

Wayne
Hobart Manor

Morristown
The Halls of Morristown:
Acorn Hall & Macculloch Hall

Bernardsville
The Bernardsville Library

CHAPTER 1

Roxana: The Ghost of Mead Hall

MADISON

ONE OF THE BEST EXAMPLES of Greek Revival architecture north of the Mason-Dixon Line, Mead Hall, on the campus of Drew University, is home to wedding receptions and gala university celebrations. Built as a residence in 1836 for William Gibbons, it was sold in 1867 to Daniel Drew, who then named it Mead Hall in honor of his wife, Roxana Mead Drew. It served as Drew Theological Seminary until 1900.

The structure was built as a "box within a box": there is about ten inches of space between the outside brick wall and the interior wall. This was a Southern design to keep the house cooler in the summer months. Unfortunately, it was this design that allowed the August 1989 fire to burn for twenty-four hours and required help from thirteen fire companies to extinguish it. The fire started from a painter's torch used to melt off old paint. Captain Lou Derosa of the Madison Fire Department said that the flame from the torch must have made its way into the space between the inside and outside walls via a carpenter bee hole.

The fire departments watered the fire from the roof and finally put it out. Amazingly, the collapse of the roof from the combined stress of fire and water pressure did not damage the beautiful oval railing on the second floor, save for a couple nicks and little burn marks. In 1991, Mead Hall received a $650,000 grant for restoration, and it reopened in 1993.

I first heard about the great fire of Mead Hall and the ghostly apparition of that event in 1996, when I was on a Halloween radio show for the local radio station WMTR 1250-AM. I was in the studio, but the other guest, Jack Rushing, had called in for the show. Jack gave historical ghost tours in the Great Swamp as well as some Revolutionary War–period cemeteries in the Morris County area.

On the air, he told the story of the fire at Mead Hall and how two firemen, one from Madison and the other from Florham Park, witnessed a woman coming toward them on the grounds outside the hall. They approached her, and one of the firemen called out to her to come to them for safety. As they got closer, they realized she was dressed in clothing from a different time period. Suddenly, she vanished right in front of them. Jack felt that this was the ghost of Roxana, the building's namesake.

In the summer of 1997, a man from Washington, D.C., contacted me and said he was filming a pilot episode for a show that he wanted to pitch to either the Discovery Channel or the Sci Fi Channel. He wanted to film Ghost Hunters Inc., which is what my then-husband and I called our little investigating firm, in action at a haunted venue. I suggested Mead Hall. The name of

this pilot was "Way Out There," an appropriate name considering it was so out there that it never aired. I'll never forget fight-
ing back my laughter as the crew donned their bright-orange
jumpsuits with the W.O.T.'s iron-on lettering on the back.

This was my first experience with a television crew on location. Up to that point, I had been on local news shows only in
the studio, at stations like News 12 NJ and CN8. I was used to
the microphone wiring and having a transmitter box clipped
to my back. What was different was having a huge boom mic
hovering over my head. Since this was my first time ghost hunting with a television crew in tow, I was uncomfortable because
we had all the lights on in Mead Hall plus all the extra lighting
of the camera crew. As they were not using infrared technology to shoot without light, I gathered that this was a low-budget
production, though I suppose I also could have looked to their
salvage-yard cars or the fact that they drove back to D.C. the
same night to eliminate hotel costs.

This was back in the days before digital photography. I didn't
get my first digital camera, a Sony Mavica, until 1999. I was using
a 35mm Pentax at the time of the Mead Hall filming. I was also
using an Aiwa boom box for collecting electronic voice phenomena (EVPs). I took some pictures as the crew finished setting up
lighting and reviewing the area for shots they wanted to film.

We started filming a walk-through beginning in the foyer.
I pointed out the two large mirrors on either side of the foyer.
Straight ahead in the hall, perpendicular to the foyer, hangs the
portrait of Roxana. A woman who works in the office at Mead
Hall told me she had witnessed a bright light coming out of Roxana's portrait, traveling to one mirror, bouncing from that mirror to the other mirror and then bouncing back to the portrait.

We made our way up the stairs and down the hall to the oval
railing. This railing surrounds the opening that allows people
on the second floor to look down on the harlequin marble foyer

and people in the foyer to look up at the skylight above the second floor. The child in me saw this more as a strategic vantage point for dropping water balloons on school officials.

Portrait of Roxana Mead Drew

As we covered the whole second floor, I took picture after picture. I used a 35mm; the instant feedback of a digital camera's LCD screen was not yet available. I shot seven rolls of film. We continued down the back stairs and covered the ballroom on the first floor. Since I had left the boom box recording for EVPs in the front room on the first floor, I made it a point to check the cassette tape to see if I needed to flip it over.

The night was wearing on, and I was getting tired and cranky from having this entourage follow me around with microphones and bright lights. I asked the producer if I could take a break. He agreed, and I went upstairs to sit on the little bench in front of the window facing the oval railing. I sat down and breathed a sigh of relief. But after a few minutes, I sensed I wasn't alone. I picked up my camera and fired off a shot at the railing. The crew noticed the flash and came running upstairs to see what happened. I told them I merely took a picture.

We proceeded to walk around the oval railing toward the hallway. I tried to take another picture, but the camera battery was dead. "I need a minute to change batteries," I said. "This one is dead."

"The battery is dead on this too," the cameraman said. "I just switched this out downstairs. This was a fully charged battery."

One by one, each person noticed their camera, recording device, anything with a battery in it, was dead. This happens on paranormal investigations. From what I can tell, the ghosts draw the energy from the batteries. It must be like an adrenaline rush for them. I explained to the television crew that a ghostly presence might have just had its power hit for the day, courtesy of our batteries. We made our way back downstairs to reload new batteries and resumed investigating upstairs, but detected no temperature fluctuations or electromagnetic fields (EMFs).

Finally, by 2:00 a.m., we completed our work and packed up. The crew was heading back to Washington D.C., and I was heading home to bed. The next day, I dropped off my seven rolls of film for developing. I sat and listened to the audio tape and heard nothing unusual. The producer called me later in the afternoon to say they had arrived safely back in D.C. They enjoyed their first ghost hunt and were looking forward to the editing process on Monday.

Monday I went back to Walgreens to pick up my pictures. I didn't even wait to get home. I sat in the parking lot reviewing the photos and was struck with disappointment. Not one orb in 168 pictures . . . but wait—there was one. That solitary orb was positioned right by the oval railing. My "ghostometer" had successfully detected a presence that night when I was on my break. I further realized that after I took this picture and the crew rushed upstairs, we all had our batteries drained.

The show never did air. I still wonder if Roxana came back to check on me when I took my break. Perhaps she was curious as to why I was finally alone. Perhaps she was making sure I wasn't disturbing anything in her home. Whatever the case, something otherworldly definitely was there that night.

A FEW YEARS LATER, I was at Drew University's Kirby Shakespeare Theatre to see the play *Enter the Guardsman*. I had heard the stories of a ghost named Reggie, who haunts the theater, which was once the campus pool. I tucked a 35mm disposable camera with 800 ISO film and a built-in flash into my purse. Reggie was a track star at the school. For some reason, while he was doing laps around the pool, he slipped, hit his head, and drowned.

During intermission, I took some pictures in the theater. After I got this film back from developing, there were two pictures with an orb in them. In the first picture, the orb was on the curtain by the stage, and in the next photo it appeared at the top of the curtain. All the photos taken after that were normal.

Maybe Reggie was doing his laps during the intermission.

The Hoyt-Bowne building on campus is where people claim to see a phantom and hear his heavy breathing. There have been reports of a piano playing when no one was there. There is also the story of a girl who was raped and killed and her ghost haunts the fourth floor of this dorm building, but I've never personally investigated this building to know for sure.

Drew University has had many politicians deliver addresses, as well as the late Christopher Reeve, who delivered the commencement speech on May 22, 1999. Yet I find it ironic that David Conrad appeared in the university's Shakespeare Festival in the summer of 2006. He plays Jim Clancy on the television show *Ghost Whisperer*. I wonder whether he knew he was performing on stage while Reggie was doing laps.

CHAPTER 2

Ladies in White
NEWARK AND TOTOWA

WHILE I'M SURE EVERY STATE HAS A GHOST STORY about a lady in white, New Jersey boasts two lady spirits clad in white: one in Branch Brook Park and the other on Riverview Drive in Totowa. Branch Brook Park (http://www.branch brookpark.org) in Newark is 360 acres of beautifully designed gardens and more than 2,000 cherry blossom trees. One can take a leisurely walk along the four miles of park. There are two three-ton stone lions, once affixed to the headquarters building of Prudential Insurance Company in downtown Newark, that stand watch over the trout-stocked lake.

Several stories surround Branch Brook's Lady in White. The

first is that she and her new husband were on their way to the park to have wedding photos taken when their limo hit a patch of ice and skidded into a tree, killing the bride instantly. A variation of that story says that in 1976 a bride and groom were on their way home from their wedding reception and the chauffeur decided to take them through Branch Brook Park. He lost control of

Branch Brook Park lion

the car on the sharp turn and the car slammed into the tree. The bride was killed, but the groom and chauffeur survived. Weeks after this crash, two other crashes took place at this same location. Another popular story has the white lady on her way to the prom with a date in the park. He lost control of his car in heavy rain and hit the same tree. The impact killed the girl, but her date escaped with minor cuts. Regardless of the discrepancies, each story says that the Lady in White lingers near the tree that caused her death. Some feel that she is warning drivers of the dangerous curve in the road. Others think she waits for her prom date to come back for her.

On a gorgeous spring day, I took a ride to Newark to search out this infamous tree. While I enjoyed the seemingly endless cherry blossoms, I couldn't find the tree of the Lady in White. I did see a couple trees with strange markings on them that could have been there to serve as an indicator of her tree, or simply a tag by the county park's official for pruning. At the south end of the park, I saw a tree with a rather odd indentation on its trunk consistent with being hit by a car. This tree, however, is no longer near the road because the county rerouted the road due to a dangerous curve near the tree. I photographed another tree, one close to the road, as an example of how the Lady in White's tree would have appeared prior to the road's rerouting.

A little background research also revealed that in 1895, much of the park was originally a swamp called Old Blue Jay Swamp. Inhabitants of the surrounding tenements drank this impure swamp water, which contributed to Newark's cholera epidemic in the 1800s. As a paranormal investigator, I suspect that the Lady in White was a product of former swamp gases and other atmospheric conditions like fog and humidity. However, the appearances of the Lady in White in Branch Brook Park seemed to subside once the road was redirected away from the fatal tree.

TOTOWA'S DEAD MAN'S CURVE

THE OTHER LADY IN WHITE is Annie of Riverview Drive in Totowa. The road runs between the Passaic River and Laurel Grove Cemetery and features a sharp bend in the road, affectionately called "Dead Man's Curve," where people say Annie was hit by a truck while walking home from the prom and dragged for fifty feet near the guardrail.

I first went to Laurel Grove Cemetery in 2000 as part of a New Jersey Ghost Hunters Society cemetery hunt. I had permission for our group to be in the cemetery. I can't stress that enough to readers who want to jump in their cars and head out to a cemetery at midnight to get permission first. Even better, explore the area during the day, and then get permission from the caretaker or, if it's a Catholic cemetery, monsignor. It's also a good idea to check in with the local police department beforehand

Branch Brook Park tree

to apprise them of what you'll be doing. If there are houses around the cemetery that you're investigating, homeowners may call the police to report flashing lights and seeing vehicles and people in the cemetery after hours.

Our Totowa group was small and manageable. I reviewed the protocols for paranormal investigating while everyone signed the waiver sheet. We synchronized our watches and agreed to search for Annie's grave and meet back at the front gate in one hour. A couple people came with me, and the others went off on their own.

We covered a lot of ground within that hour. I remember taking one orb picture at a mausoleum. Other people captured some orb shots at various locations in the cemetery, but nothing stellar. EMF and temperature readings were normal. No one reported collecting any EVPs, and Annie's grave eluded us.

After an hour we convened with the other part of the group, and I took attendance to make sure everyone was accounted for. One gentleman suggested we drive the length of Riverview Drive to see if Annie would appear. I agreed since our cars were all facing in that direction anyway. I knew the street would bend down to the right to follow the Passaic River, make a sharp turn and continue back out to the main road. I stressed to the team that we were only going to make the trip once. It was a residential area, and I didn't want our caravan to be a nuisance.

We got in our cars and made our funeral-procession-paced drive down Riverview. As we were passing the cemetery on our right and the Passaic River on our left, I put my passenger window down and hung out a little to take pictures. I call this method "drive-by shooting." I didn't capture anything of a paranormal nature, but I have to say that it is a creepy road to drive along.

Once we were back on the main drag, we made the traditional stop at the first diner we saw. With digital cameras we were able to review and compare our cemetery hunt pictures over coffee and fries with melted mozzarella cheese and gravy. There were some interesting orb shots, but no full-body apparitions and certainly no Annie appearance. I asked whether anyone saw the blood-red paint on the guardrail that supposedly marks where Annie was hit and killed the night of her prom. Everyone admitted it was too dark to see any paint, if it was there. The eerie red paint is part of the legend that Annie's father returns here on the eve of the anniversary of her death to repaint the guardrail.

A few months later, on a Sunday afternoon, my then-husband and I were in Totowa with our hearse, Baby, to attend a Cadillac car show at the Brogan Cadillac dealership. There were many classic Cadillacs, but ours was the only hearse. After the show, we headed for Riverview Drive and noticed some splattered red paint on the road, but did not see any on the guardrail. I figured this was the act of a teenager wanting to spook his girlfriend on their midnight ride home. Of course, I think we spooked the oncoming car even more as our twenty-two-foot-long hearse came around the corner of "Dead Man's Curve."

In May 2008 I went up to Laurel Grove Cemetery to take a daytime picture of the entrance sign. Afterward, my sons and I hopped back in my car to make the drive down Riverview and look for the red paint on the guardrail. Sadly, the road was closed for construction. The site looked like an additional bridge was being built across the Passaic River. Oddly enough, this new bridge appears to start where Annie ended. Who knows? This may be the beginning of another legendary ghost-girl-on-the-bridge story.

L'Aura with son Trent in Laurel Grove Cemetery

CHAPTER 3

The Ghost of Rose City

MADISON

I GREW UP IN MADISON, NEW JERSEY, also known as the Rose City, went to school at St. Vincent the Martyr on Green Village Avenue, and spent summers hanging out at the playground at the end of Delbarton Drive. There was a path from this park through the woods that had the best blackberries. The path led to Memorial Park, where I learned to ice skate.

I have fond memories of growing up in Madison. The city provided the nation's best hotels with fresh roses. And to this day, I am an Italian-food snob. Having been brought up with Mrs. Coviello's manicotti and Mrs. Massucci's homemade pizza, I see the Olive Garden's offerings as "plastic Italian." In addition to the great food and the not-so-great beatings I took for my younger brother from members of "the Niles gang," neighborhood teens from Niles Avenue, there was this scary story my mother used to tell me about the ghost of a young girl who was murdered on the way home from her baby-sitting job.

In early adulthood I forgot about the story as I concentrated on my family and career. However, once I turned back to my interest in the paranormal, primarily ghost hunting, I asked my mother more about it. Mom said that when she was a teller at the Madison National Bank, there was a part-time teller named Whitney Atchison. Whitney served in the Navy on an aircraft carrier during the Vietnam War. A tire blew out on one of the planes, striking Whitney and costing him his arm and leg. He knew the ghost-girl story and would discuss it with my mom. He claimed his grandfather was on the Madison police force when the murder happened.

Mom said that over the years motorists would report seeing a young girl walking on Ridgedale Avenue who would then vanish. I was intrigued. My research at the Morris County Library turned up the year of the murder, 1921. Armed with that information, I found many articles on microfiche at the library relating to the murder of a girl named Jeanette Lawrence.

Jeanette, who was twelve, lived at 142 Ridgedale Avenue with her mother, father, and sixteen-year-old brother. She was in seventh grade at Green Avenue School and baby-sat Mrs. Sandt's four-year-old daughter, Madeline, on a regular basis. The Sandts lived around the corner, at 19 Fairview Avenue. On October 6 of that year, at around 5:30 p.m., Jeanette left Mrs. Sandt's house to return home. When Jeanette turned around to wave good-bye, it was the last time Mrs. Sandt would see her alive.

It should have taken about ten minutes for Jeanette to walk home. When she did not arrive home at the usual time, Mrs. Lawrence sent her son to Mrs. Sandt's house to see if Jeanette was still there. Mrs. Sandt explained that Jeanette had left a half hour earlier. Mr. Lawrence and his son grabbed flashlights and proceeded to search the immediate neighborhood calling out for Jeanette. Neighbors pitched in on the search, and by 7:00 p.m. the Madison Police were contacted. Even the local Boy Scout troop pitched in to search for Jeanette since her family and the police feared the girl might have fallen and been injured in the brush while traversing the Kluxen Woods. In fact, two Boy Scouts, Chauncey Griswold and Walter Schultz, found Jeanette's body in Kluxen Woods. Her wrists had been bound behind her back with floral twine, which was readily available given all the nurseries in town. Her body had twenty-three stab wounds, and police later determined that Jeanette had been sexually assaulted.

As the investigation ensued, police learned that Francis Peter Kluxen III, a troubled fourteen-year-old, had bullied Jeanette on at least several occasions. Francis had become too much trouble for the nuns to handle and was expelled from St. Vincent's, my school. He was taken into custody and questioned. His mother raised suspicion by soaking the pants Francis had worn the day

Map of Jeanette Lawrence's neighborhood

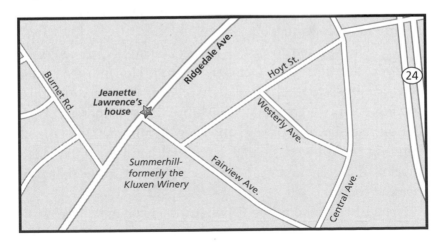

of Jeanette's murder, stating that he had wine stains on them from working at the family's winery. Forensics in that era were not able to detect bloodstains following the washing.

Strangely, Mr. Monell Sayre, a wealthy resident of Convent Station, persuaded Francis's parents to let him adopt the boy and make him the sole heir to Sayre's estate. By the time Francis was brought to trial in July 1922, he was fifteen years old, stood six feet two inches, and weighed 170 pounds.

Francis appeared to have been well-prepared for his testimony on the witness stand, and he narrated his version of what happened the evening of the murder with a charming composure that won over the jury. It deliberated for just three hours before acquitting him. Many people in Madison thought he was guilty as sin and that Sayre had bought Francis's freedom with high-powered defense attorneys.

In 1926, Francis Peter Kluxen III left Madison for San Diego. He attacked and robbed two men with a meat cleaver on Christmas Day 1932. He also shot and killed a San Diego neighbor in June 1933. The coroner determined that Francis, by this time a twenty-seven-year-old Marine officer, acted in self-defense. By April 1934, San Diego police had charged him in nine burglaries and recovered $1,000 worth of stolen property from his residence. He served time in San Quentin before dying in San Francisco in 1971.

Jeanette was laid to rest at her grandparents' cemetery in Andover, New Jersey, on October 14, 1921. Her murder is still listed as "unsolved," and motorists claim to see a young girl walking down the road and vanishing. Some witnesses claim that they see her turn, wave, and then disappear. This type of haunting could be considered a residual haunting—the video imprint of the last living moments of Jeanette's life that play over and over.

When I returned to the Chatham/Madison area, I held the

monthly meetings of the NJGHS at the Madison Public Library. After one meeting, a woman approached me and asked if I knew anything about a haunting in Madison. I told her about the Jeanette Lawrence case. She said that her son saw the ghost of a girl in their home. Their house is on Central Avenue, directly across the street from Summerhill Park, whose main entrance is on Ridgedale Avenue. Summerhill also once held the Kluxen Winery. It was closed, and its parts auctioned off, in 1972.

The woman was not sure that she wanted an investigation of her home as she was renting the place and afraid her landlord would not approve. Luckily, her son was with her, so I was able to ask him some questions about his experience. He told me that he saw a girl around his age, eleven or so. He said he saw

Orb at Kluxen Woods

"Kluxen Woods"
Orb shot - Nicole D.
5/15/04

her once in the dining room and once going down the hall and vanishing though a wall. I suggested that they conduct their own investigation by taking pictures and audio recordings.

As part of the NJ Ghost Conference 2004, I took a group to Summerhill Park for an investigation. In the dark, it was too dangerous to climb down the remains of the steps of the winery. One attendee, Nichole, did capture an amazing orb photo. I did register a drop in temperature, only about ten degrees, in the area where Nichole took this picture. There were several faint orbs, which might have been dust or pollen, but there were also two very bright orbs. One is smaller than the other. This could be explained by depth of field, but it could also be representative of Jeanette and Francis because she was so much smaller than he was. Other than this photo, no EVPs were recorded on our digital audio equipment nor EMFs detected on the meters.

I would love to drive along Ridgedale Avenue and survey Summerhill Park some October 6, the anniversary of Jeanette's murder, and find out which spots she favors and whether she's still trying to explain to the living the truth about what happened.

CHAPTER 4

Lambert Castle

PATERSON

THIS CASTLE DOES NOT HAVE A TREACHEROUS
APPROACH along the Carpathian Mountains, nor does it
have a sinister owner like Count Dracula. This castle was constructed in 1892 by the "Silk Baron" of "Silk City," Catholina
Lambert, who came to America from England in 1851, when
he was seventeen years old. His successful business ventures
allowed him to build his own castle atop Garret Mountain in
Paterson. He and his wife, Isabella Shattuck, had seven children. He collected art and displayed it in the castle's three-story
atrium. In fact, when he fell into debt later in life, selling pieces

Stained glasss window of Florence Lambert

from his collection allowed him to live in the castle comfortably until his death in 1923.

Before beginning the self-guided tour of the castle, I spoke with the docents on duty, members of the Passaic County Historical Society. Of course, I had to ask if they had had any paranormal experiences while volunteering at the castle. Both women said they hadn't but that the director might have some experiences to share. He wasn't in, so I left my card in hopes he would contact me. He never did. Historical society people are either "hot" or "cold" about the idea of ghosts. There is no in between. I don't take offense to their perception in either case.

The first docent I spoke with mentioned that all seven of the Lambert children had died. The longest-living child was Florence, who died at the age of twenty-four. She was married and had given birth to one child but died of pneumonia shortly thereafter. She is fondly remembered as the Biblical character Rebecca in the stained glass window on the landing of the main staircase.

I had my sons with me on this visit, so I was hopeful that I might capture an EVP or two, given the deaths of the children. There were a couple of times that we were secluded from other castle visitors and I was able to record. I even prompted my younger son to say, "Come play with us." He did a good impression of the ghostly girls from *The Shining*, but it wasn't enough to attract any phantom children.

When we came out of the castle, three large turkey vultures landed on the grass just below where I had my car parked, an ominous sight in spite of the clear and sunny day. I had to drive past the vultures for my sons to get a closer look. As we went down the drive, we saw a dead squirrel on the side of the road. He was not crushed. He appeared intact and was lying on his back with his mouth open. There was a little trail of blood trickling from his mouth. I wasn't sure if the turkey vultures portended the dead squirrel we saw, or if he was certain to be their next snack. Either way, the vultures and squirrel gave us a macabre adrenaline rush.

We drove around to see the tower that Lambert built in 1896 for a 360-degree view of the Paterson region and the New York City skyline in the distance. The self-tour pamphlet notes that in WWII the tower was used to monitor the skies for enemy war planes. This tower was accessible by the public until the 1960s, when it was deemed unsafe. The tower is now being renovated and will reopen to the public. I think it would be interesting to do some EVP work in this tower given its age and the renovations.

From here, we drove to Garret Mountain Reservation. This is home to the seventy-seven-foot Great Falls of the Passaic River. It's said that a ghost sometimes can be seen coming through the mists of the falls, suspected to be the spectral remains of a suicide victim. It was also the site of a military encampment during the Revolutionary War. People claim to see a Revolutionary soldier limping along the side of the road, holding his arm.

Garret Mountain Reservation is a scenic park with shady places to pull the car over and just relax. I was telling my sons about "Elvis" performing here on a stage he sets up himself. Sadly, we didn't find him, but if you check *Weird N.J.* magazine, issue no. 29, page 57, you'll see his picture.

Lambert Castle tower

Of course this park is not without its legend of the madman who terrorized parked cars along "Lovers' Lane" in the 1950s and 1960s. I could see this being a perfect spot to park the car and make out above the city lights. I can also understand how such a terror tale might be produced by the overactive imaginations of young people. The story goes that a patient in a nearby psychiatric facility escaped and made his way to Garret Mountain. He had a prosthetic hook for his left hand. He mounted the hood of one of the parked cars and frightened the couple inside. The young man put the car in reverse and sped backward hoping to dislodge the "psycho hood ornament." After the young man backed up and then stopped the car abruptly to go forward and exit the park, the escapee fell off the car. When the couple arrived at the girl's home, they were shocked to find the hook stuck in the passenger's car door handle.

Having a conversation with one of the volunteers at the castle was interesting. Although she had not experienced anything paranormal, she said she would not want to spend the night alone in the place! She told me that if she were forced to remain there all night, snowbound, for example, she would have every light in the place turned on. I can empathize. The place is overwhelming in the daytime. I wouldn't want to be there at night either.

This volunteer was kind enough to substantiate her apprehensive feelings by telling me of a fellow volunteer's encounter. One night when this volunteer was locking up the castle, she was going from room to room on each floor checking for remaining visitors. She worked her way down to the main floor. As she stepped off the staircase to return to the reception desk, she saw a man out of the corner of her eye. As she turned to get a better look, she saw the man crossing the atrium. She followed him to ask him to leave. But as she entered the atrium, she noticed a cold chill in the air. There was no one there. She walked the perimeter of the atrium and could not find the man she had just seen walking through. It was then she realized why the man appeared familiar to her. She'd seen his portrait: it was Catholina Lambert.

The park is closed from sundown to sunrise and therefore not legally accessible to investigate at night. However, people have seen the Revolutionary War soldier at dusk limping along the road toward the park exit. I suggest taking the tour of Lambert Castle and recording for EVPs if you can be secluded from other tourists. Then, drive on to Garret Mountain Reservation and enjoy some Elvis songs. As the sun sets, head slowly toward the park exit, and do some "drive-by shooting." While one person drives, the passenger can aim the camera out the window. Ready, aim, fire!

CHAPTER 5

The Whistling Swan Inn
STANHOPE

THE WHISTLING SWAN INN is a beautiful Victorian house built circa 1905 that is now a splendid bed and breakfast in Stanhope. I had heard that it is haunted when I was investigating Bell's Mansion (see Chapter 7), also in Stanhope. I followed up with Liz Armstrong, the owner of the Whistling Swan and ended up booking a dinner and investigation event here on October 2, 2004, for the NJGHS.

Liz said she had had some weird experiences since purchasing the inn in 2001. Her fiancé found a little red-handled hatchet on his workbench in the basement. He asked Liz if she had put it there, but she said no. They had no idea how it got there. Another time, her housekeeper's children were playing in the front yard while their mother was inside cleaning. The kids came in calling to their mother to see what she wanted. The housekeeper said she had not called them in, but the children said they saw a woman in the upstairs window waving to them. They thought it was their mother.

I'll never forget the night of the dinner and investigation. I was sick as a dog. Between the migraine and the upset stomach that accompanied it, I spent more time in the bathroom than I did investigating the inn. I did manage to take a picture of an orb on the piano in the front parlor, though. Dina Chirico, team leader for the Northwest Division of the NJGHS, captured the orb in motion by the piano on her still-frame camera too.

A married couple who are NJGHS members were staying at the inn for the event and the weekend. The husband told me that earlier in the afternoon he had tried to incite the female spirit that supposedly haunts the room they rented. He said he screamed all kinds of profanity to get the spirit to show herself or at least give a sign of her presence. Dead or alive, women don't like being cursed and yelled at, so what was he thinking? I clued him in to the protocols of investigating and reiterated the one about "no spirit provocation."

The investigation continued with a journey to the inn's basement. I took a photo of an orb on the stairs leading to the basement. In the basement, there were a couple of sectioned-off rooms. Liz's fiancé used one of these as his work area—that's where he found the hatchet resting on his workbench. The group took turns going in and out of these little rooms to take photos and thermal readings and to scan for EMF. An investigator claimed to psychically pick up a man who was very abusive to his wife and would lock her in these "torture" rooms. While it makes for an ideal television script, no research ever validated an incident of that sort on the property.

The evening concluded with everyone pleased with the dinner, the venue, and their ghost hunt. Again, a couple orb pictures were captured during this investigation, but nothing more
substantial in the way of EVP or video.

The NJGHS returned to the Whistling Swan Inn the next
year with the television crew from a local cable show, *Neighborhood Journal*. Brian Sandt, NJGHS's technical advisor, was the
team leader on this investigation. They did not detect much in
the way of ghostly activity while there, but Gregory Irish, team
leader for the Central Jersey Division of the NJGHS, noted a loud
bang that came from one of the guest rooms as he approached
it. He attempted to replicate the sound but couldn't, nor could
he explain how it happened. He also took a picture of an orb in
front of and above Dina Chirico, Team Leader of the North Jersey Division of the NJGHS, in the basement.

Dina captured an EVP while standing near the entrance to
the Walnut Valley Suite on the second floor. She asked, "Can you
tell us your name? Are you male or female?" She did not hear
a response. While doing her data review from the evening, she
heard a female's voice whispering on the tape, "Go in there."

A few days following the on-location taping, Tom Lupo, producer of *Neighborhood Journal*, contacted me to say that while
editing the show, he saw something he could not figure out.
He was filming Brian in the basement conducting a routine
EMF sweep. In the lower right-hand corner of the video frame,
there's an amorphous black shadow. It manifests and dissipates
very quickly, but is certainly noticeable. Brian did not detect any
unusual EMF readings, and he was disappointed that "it" was
right behind him and he didn't even know it.

Tom told me he ran through the footage repeatedly and
called in several of his colleagues to watch it to see if they could
provide an explanation for the shadow. They were all at a loss

to define or explain this shadow. I've watched this clip several times, and I can't explain it. Given the bright light on the Hi-8 camera that he was using to film Brian, it's physically impossible for this shadow to appear where and how it does in the frame.

I find this to be the best evidence of ghosts since Tom was not holding his camera as a ghost hunter in search of life beyond the grave. He was holding his camera as television producer filming for his television show. Yet he captured the best anomaly of the entire investigation.

In early 2008, I followed up with Liz Armstrong about any other unusual occurrences. She said, "It's been pretty quiet here." I asked if any guests reported anything out of the ordinary, and again her answer was no. It could be that the spirits have settled in with Liz. She's been the owner of the bed and breakfast for seven years now. Sometimes changes in ownership and renovations to a house or building can bring otherwise latent spirits to the fore. This home was originally constructed as a gift for Sarah, the wife of Daniel Best, who was the Justice of the Peace in 1905. I find it interesting that when Liz took over the Whistling Swan Inn, she was engaged. This might have given her an emotional connection to Daniel, given his occupation when he was alive at this house. The emotional connection is another trigger that can bring ghosts out of the woodwork. For example, an elderly couple sells their home of fifty years and moves away. The new owners are a family with young children. The elderly couple didn't experience any paranormal activity while living at the house, but the new owners hear the sounds of children playing when they know their kids are at school. The children complain of not being able to sleep at night because the "little girl and boy want to play." The children's ghosts were in the house the whole time the elderly couple lived there, but did not connect with them. They are children and therefore feel a bond or connection with the children who have moved into the house.

This leads me to believe that the Whistling Swan Inn is worth the visit. You just might be the person who has a connection with one of the spirits residing there. If nothing else, you will enjoy a reprieve from the stress of work and commuting, and the bed and breakfast's beauty and tranquility.

CHAPTER 6

The Stanhope House
STANHOPE

THE STANHOPE HOUSE IS KNOWN for "presenting the finest musical artists in various genres to include bluegrass, rock, folk and America's indigenous musical art form . . . the blues," as the Web site says. Of course, given its two hundred-year history, it's also acquired a few permanent performers—ghosts. Sadly, as this book goes to print, the Stanhope House has closed its doors due to litigation problems the owners are experiencing. I was told by the former manager, Amy Connolly, that they are in a "wait and see" holding pattern pending the litigation. Hopefully her brother, one of the partners/owners, will secure complete control of the Stanhope House and re-open it. Given the prized liquor license that is part of Stanhope House, Amy is confident it will re-open as a bar and restaurant no matter what.

Its history dates to an American colonist who made the original land acquisition in 1789. The structure was built in 1790. If you look closely at the top of the joining beams, you'll see Roman numerals carved in them. This reveals the method of assembly at a time when there were no blueprints. The beams were hand carved, numbered, and joined via tongue and groove, a longtime patron and employee of the Stanhope House, Bobby, told me. The house has served as a town hall, complete with jail and post office; a library; and as a major stagecoach stop on the Morris and Sussex Turnpike. It morphed into a hotel—and some say a brothel—and was the last stop on the Morris Canal. During Prohibition, there was a secret bar in the basement. While the Morris Canal was operating, Stanhope House had two bars: the main one and the "puller's bar." The puller's bar was for canal workers who pulled boats with the help of mules. Having an offensive odor was an occupational hazard, so they were sequestered.

I learned about the possible haunting of the Stanhope House from my cousin's wife who frequented the place when she lived up the street. She directed me to the then-owner, Maureen. I contacted Maureen because I was looking for a venue, preferably a haunted one, to record our two Halloween episodes of the podcast *The Deadline.* Maureen agreed to let us record on October 25. Although she would not be available that evening, she said her daughter, Mary, would be able to meet with us and give an interview on the show.

Maureen told me that several times she had heard a female singing in the sound booth. The sound engineer would hear the singing too. She also said that she would catch shadows of people out of the corner of her eye even when she knew for a fact that she was alone.

It was a nasty night weather-wise for our recording at the Stanhope House. Rain and fog made the short drive seem endless. Once inside, it was quite cozy and low key as no bands were performing. It was Texas Hold 'Em night. So aside from the occasional outbursts of happy winners, it was relatively easy to record the shows. Brian Sandt, NJGHS technical advisor and producer of *The Deadline*, had already had his dinner (the New York strip steak) and set up the podcast equipment and microphones by the time I arrived. I set out the T-shirts, bumper stickers, and flyers as information and prizes for interested passers-by. David Rountree, of Skylands Paranormal Investigations and a fellow NJGHS member, was also there to contribute to the show.

Mary, Maureen's daughter, came by for our first show and told us of her ghostly experiences while working at the Stanhope House. She tended bar and managed the place. She was a bright, down-to-earth type of woman who said that she would see the shadow of someone walking by the bar but when she would lift her head to look for the person, no one would be there. She also said she would have the distinct feeling of someone behind her, so strong that if she was washing the glasses at the bar she would shift over for the person to pass by her. Then she would realize no one was trying to get past her. I asked Mary if she experienced this when the bar was open and busy. "No," she said. "It happens mostly when it's not crowded in here."

Mary's most eerie experience happened in the sound booth, which was enclosed at one time. She showed us where the walls used to be. She said she was inside speaking with the sound engineer when she heard a female singing. She looked up at the stage to see if someone was doing a sound check but no one was there. She then looked at the engineer and said, "Did you hear that?" He turned to her and said, "Oh you finally heard her?" Up to that point, Mary hadn't believed her mother, who heard this female voice singing on several occasions.

On one occasion, the lead singer of a band that was performing on stage witnessed a ghostly replay of a murder. Being a professional, he managed to finish the set. Once he got off stage, he went straight to Maureen and said, "You're not going to believe what I just saw—a murder!" Maureen remained calm. "Yeah that really happened here," she said. Apparently two men brawled, and one ended up killing the other.

Mary told us that about ten or eleven years prior, her cousin, Chuck, was the manager of the Stanhope House. He was a bachelor and a bit of a Casanova in that he had a different girlfriend every week. The upstairs was a rooming house. He lived in one of the rooms at the end of the hall, and the remaining rooms were for bands to stay in during their scheduled performances. One band's lead diva, E. C. Scott, was returning to her room when she saw a young woman walk into Chuck's room. E. C. decided to knock on his door and, upon his answering, asked him to introduce her to his girlfriend. Chuck explained to her that he had no girlfriend and was completely alone in his room. She was not happy with this answer and made Chuck walk with her throughout the building searching for this young woman. After satisfying her that there was no one else there, Chuck asked, "What did this girl look like?" E. C. described the woman. Chuck laughed and said, "Oh, that was a ghost you saw!" This was very unsettling to E. C. She woke up her band members and made them gather in her room to stand guard over her so she could sleep.

Mary told me that her mom had seen this young woman many times walking in the main area of the bar, but never upstairs where E. C. encountered her.

Another possible spirit at Stanhope House is that of the bartender who hanged himself from the rafters in the late 1960s. To this day, some customers buy him a drink and leave it on the bar for him. I asked Mary if she knew the details of this suicide, such as why he did himself in, but she said she did not.

Bobby first came to the Stanhope House about twenty years ago to enjoy the bands and party life. In 2004, he heard the owner was planning to renovate the place, and he asked whether he could be a part of that project. He was hired. Bobby not only worked to complete those renovations, but he remained on staff as a handyman and jack of all trades. He helps out wherever he's needed.

While renovating, Bobby says the owner bought him a hammer, but Bobby didn't like it because it was too small and light. Four days after he got it, the hammer went missing. Bobby said he looked everywhere but couldn't find it. He continued with his work of ripping up the bathroom floors. Three days later he went to cut some plumbing in the bathroom. In order to do this, he had to remove a portion of the flooring. There he found the hammer. It was difficult to comprehend how the hammer got there since the floor had been intact until that point. The guy Bobby was working with was completely spooked and maintained that one of the other workers was playing a joke on them. That would be plausible except why would someone rip up a floor, place a hammer in the hole, and then put the floor back together?

Bobby pointed out the 200-year-old stairs propped up against the wall behind the bar. They were the original steps of the building when it was a hotel. He sometimes hears them creaking even though they're mainly used to display beer bottles now. He also said that in the 1960s, the renovations included tearing down the stairwell to the basement. Inside the walls, wrapped in burlap, they discovered guns from the Civil War in mint condition. These were sold for approximately $100,000. As for the "secret bar" during Prohibition, Bobby said during renovations they uncovered tins that were buried in the dirt floor of the basement. The tins were used to hide liquor. Sadly, they were empty.

Babe Ruth used to frequent this "secret bar."

After our podcast trip, Brian and David eventually went back when the bar was closed to investigate the Stanhope House with an Internet vidcast crew in tow. Brian said he didn't capture anything he would deem paranormal. David, however, said he had chronic problems with the handheld oscilloscope he used to capture EMF waveforms. He said it kept turning off every five minutes even though the batteries were brand new. Dave also documented some EMF spikes over at the murder scene by the stage. Dave collected a couple of orb photos that he concluded were dust orbs, but he did capture an EVP of "help me" over by the former sound booth. Unfortunately this was lost when his computer crashed.

In 2008, I spoke with the manager of the Stanhope House, Amy Connolly. In the short time her brother, Matthew Williams, and his partner, Richard Urmston, have owned the venue, she's had a couple of strange experiences. First she told me that she had arrived around 5:00 p.m. to open the Stanhope House one evening. This was in the late fall, and it was already getting dark outside. As she was fumbling for the key to unlock the door, she could hear the television on inside. When she walked in, the television on the far right side of the bar was on but then shut itself off. She figured Mike Burtnick, the sound engineer whose car was in the parking lot, was playing a joke on her. She called out for him, expecting him to jump up from behind the bar and yell "Boo!" but he did not answer her. She continued walking in and calling for Mike, but no one answered her.

Amy found a cocktail napkin on the bar in front of a bar stool that would be in perfect position for watching the television that had just shut off. She knew she had cleaned off the bar completely the night before when she closed up and thought it odd that she missed this napkin. As she threw the napkin in the trash, her cell phone rang. It was Mike saying that he was with her brother on an errand. She told him what happened and that she thought he was playing a trick on her. They had a good laugh about it, and that was that. Or so she thought. Amy continued to make her way around the place turning on lights and setting up. When she came back to the bar, another cocktail napkin was on the bar in the exact place as before. She again threw it out. Later that night, as the business was winding down, another cocktail napkin appeared in the same spot on the bar. Amy jokes that is her "steady ghost customer."

All of the bartenders, according to Amy, have heard footsteps in the empty rooms above the bar. These rooms have not been occupied since the Stanhope House ceased being a boarding house. Mike, the sound engineer, shared with me that he's closed the door that leads to the room where the bartender hanged himself only to find it open again ten minutes later. He said he's had this happen several times. He also said he gets a "creeped out" feeling when he is there alone and closing up.

Amy said she caught a glimpse of the young woman ghost when she was cleaning up the green room, where the performers hang out before and between sets. Amy swore she saw a young woman walk through the double-door entrance into the bar area. Amy went to see who it was as the bar was closed and no customers should have been in the building at the time. No one was there. Amy said she returned to the green room and again she caught the same person out of the corner of her eye repeating the same steps through the entrance way and into the bar. Amy proceeded to inspect the bar once more and again found no one there.

So, if you're looking for an entertaining weekend getaway complete with ghosts, combine a trip to the Stanhope House with a stay at the Whistling Swan Inn (Chapter 5) and dinner at Bell's Mansion (Chapter 7). All are within walking distance of each other. Enjoy!

Bell's Mansion

STANHOPE

BELL'S MANSION TODAY IS A THRIVING RES-
TAURANT in Stanhope. Chef Martin Kowalski has created a
menu packed with mouth-watering delights. And after taking
a seat at the gorgeous bar, built in the late 1800s for the Palm-
erton Hotel in Pennsylvania, one can enjoy a wide selection of
top-shelf spirits.

The house itself was constructed between 1835 and 1840 by
Robert P. Bell. He was wealthy and owned various mills in addition to being president of the Morris Canal & Banking Company. His mansion's view of the Morris Canal was the product

of fellow Morristown businessman George Macculloch. Many parks still permit public access to this historic, 102-mile canal throughout Warren and Morris counties.

Bell's Mansion went through several owners after Robert Bell but remained in the Salmon family the longest. Herbert Salmon bought the mansion in 1905 and died there in 1977, at the age of 99. The house fell into decay during the 1980s and 1990s until it was purchased by Bob and Jean Duda in 2001. They went on to create their living quarters on the second floor and designed the restaurant and bar on the first floor.

A few years ago I went to have dinner and investigate the restaurant with a friend of mine, Nichole. As a young girl, Nichole, along with her brother, sneaked into the mansion while it was vacant and decaying. A Stanhope native, Nichole had been at summer camp one year when she heard a girl from a completely different town tell a story about the doll that was supposedly in the attic of the Bell's Mansion. Nichole and her brother were on a mission to retrieve that fabled doll when they were caught. She said that they got as far as the main foyer and were about to go up the stairs when a caretaker who lived nearby saw their bicycles near the house and escorted them from the premises.

Actually, Nichole was lucky that the caretaker made them leave when he did. The staircase they were about to ascend was in shambles, and they stood a good chance of falling through it and being severely injured, with no way to get help.

Nichole told me the haunted doll story over dinner. Skeptic that I am, I listened intently while classifying the story in my head as an urban legend. But I admit it makes for a great summer campfire ghost story, and it goes like this: One day a young engaged couple came to see the lovely Bell's Mansion and decided to purchase it to live in after their wedding. The young lady moved in and began to fix it up while her fiancé continued to live at his premarital address. Her fiancé was away on a business trip during her bridal shower, but she received many gifts, one of which was a beautiful porcelain doll. She had the gifts in her car to get them home, but she did not want to damage the porcelain doll, so she kept that on the front seat with her while she drove home. On the way, she swore she heard the doll say to her, "Don't go through with the wedding! Something terrible will happen." The bride-to-be wrote this off to being exhausted from the long bridal shower.

Once she was home, she unloaded the gifts into the house and took the doll up to her bedroom. While she ran her shower and prepared to get ready for bed, she heard the doll issue its warning once more: "Don't go through with the wedding! Something terrible will happen." At this point, she grabbed the doll and took it up to the attic and left it there. She never mentioned the bizarre warning to her fiancé, and they were married as planned. They had a lovely ceremony and hit the dance floor at their reception for their first dance as husband and wife. As they swirled around and around, gazing into each other's eyes, the large chandelier above them came crashing down. They were killed instantly.

When Nichole brought up the story to the owners' daughter, Tracey, she claimed that she had been up in the attic when they were renovating and no such doll was ever found.

Tracey introduced us to her parents, Bob and Jean Duda. They were kind enough to let us into their private living quarters upstairs. I took some digital pictures and captured an orb in one bedroom.

Bob was skeptical of the ghostly phenomena but accepting of the stories he had heard from his wife and his wait staff. In fact, Jean had her prime ghost encounter while seated at the bar one evening with Bob right there. They were talking with the bartender when Jean felt a hand on her upper back. She described it as being a light, open-handed pressure between her shoulder blades as if someone were either trying to get her attention or to squeeze in between her and Bob to place a drink order. She turned around to see who it was and found no one there.

We made our way down to the basement. It has a huge cistern along with storage racks, extra dining chairs, and racks with various canned goods and catering supplies. I managed to capture an orb at one end of this area and again at the opposite end under the stairwell.

The other side of the basement was more peaceful. This was the family's storage area. Old toys, holiday decorations, and furniture were stored here. I didn't capture any orb anomalies, but definitely felt the "creep factor" in this area.

Nichole and I concluded the night was a success. She was thrilled by the fact that her childhood dream of exploring the mansion had finally become reality. She covered every inch of the mansion, save for the attic. Amidst patrons, waiters, bar room music and general restaurant chaos, I captured two orbs with my camera; that was impressive.

In September of that same year, my team from the NJGHS and I went to investigate Bell's Mansion more formally. We were being filmed for a local cable TV show called *Neighborhood Journal*. This time we met the Dudas there on a Monday evening, when the restaurant was closed.

It was a hot and humid Indian summer night, with camera lights making it even hotter. Thankfully, we got through that part rather quickly and got down to ghost-hunting business.

The TV crew interviewed Matthew Lott, a server at the restaurant. He told them about the night he was cleaning off some tables in the Canal Room after closing. The room used to be a porch but was enclosed to serve as a dining room. As he was cleaning this particular table, he looked up through a window to the adjoining small dining room, and he saw a woman sitting at a table staring out toward the parking lot. He watched her for a good ten seconds and then entered the dining room to ask her to leave since the restaurant was closed. By the time he reached her table, she had disappeared. The only way out of the dining room was the very doorway he had just passed through. He didn't see or hear anyone go by him or down the hallway. She simply vanished. He came out of the dining room and was very shaken. Bob recalls that Matt was "as white as a ghost." Yes, Bob added the disclaimer "no pun intended."

Bob noted that he's had several other busboys witness this female ghost and turn in their aprons abruptly, without another job to go to.

We needed to re-create this scene for the television show. One of our team members, Sherry Irish, was kind enough to let me put up her hair and dress her in the costume that best brought to life the ghostly image that Matt witnessed. Prior to filming Sherry's debut as a female ghost, NJGHS technical advisor Brian Sandt recorded some unusual EMF readings in this dining room. Team member Dina Chirico took pictures of Brian while he was scanning with the EMF meter. In one picture, a small orb appeared right next to the word "ghosts?" on the back of Brian's NJGHS T-shirt. Team member Gregory Irish also photographed this orb along the floor and two others by the fireplace with his digital camera. For a paranormal investigator, it's a mark of achievement when more than one device picks up an anomaly concurrently.

We concluded the investigation and spent the next several days reviewing our data. The orb pictures could not be disqualified as dust or pollen. There were several frames before and after each of these orb shots that had no such anomalies. No EVPs were collected.

Many people have made the pilgrimage to the Haunted Mansion in Disney's theme parks. Bell's Mansion is not as holographically infested but is definitely not as pricey to get into. It's well worth the trip for a great meal and a chance to dine along with a real ghost. Bon appétit!

CHAPTER 8

Shades of Death Road and Ghost Lake

LIBERTY, INDEPENDENCE, AND ALLANUCHY

SHADES OF DEATH ROAD IN WARREN COUNTY winds above the fertile sod farms of Great Meadows. The road was originally called Shades Road because of the tall trees that line it and, in full bloom, create an amazing, shady canopy. It's a beautiful drive for five miles on a sunny Sunday afternoon, yet it takes on a more foreboding atmosphere at night.

There are many tales about this stretch of road. The first is that the ghostlike wisps of fog so common on the road are the spirits of the Indians who died along it. True, the Lenni Lenape Indians staggered home from their battle at the Delaware with the Iroquois of New York. Those who did not die in battle succumbed to malaria from the mosquitoes that bit them while they traversed this route. The fog, however, is simply an atmospheric manifestation of ground and water warmed during the day colliding with the cool night air.

49

The deadliness of the road became well known to the locals. People avoided the area for fear of contracting malaria. This made it a perfect refuge for the criminal element. They would rather contend with a disease than be captured and brought to justice. In the 1800s, a man and his horse were found dead on Shades Road, apparently the victims of a robbery. In the 1930s, another robbery victim was bludgeoned to death with the jack handle of his Ford Model T. In both cases, the murderers were never caught.

Ghost Lake was created by a dam that was built between adjoining properties owned by William Crouse Jr. and Leon Hull in the 1940s. Therefore, the tale of Indian spirits rising from the waters of Ghost Lake cannot be true, given the obvious glitch in timing. Crouse and Hull chose this area to build their stately homes specifically because of the addresses, which by that time were officially on Shades of Death Road. They realized that the negative reputation of the road gave them the benefits of privacy and solitude. They not only named their newly formed lake "Ghost Lake," but they also called their properties "Haunted Hollow" and the mountain "Murderer's Mountain."

While I'm punching holes in the romantic ghost tales, let me continue with the one about the ghostly bride and groom whose spirits are seen rising from the depths of Ghost Lake. It's a great campfire story of the bride and groom rowing out to the center of the lake on their wedding night for a private moonlit toast of champagne. The bride got tipsy and fell into the lake. The weight of her wedding gown pulled her down and held her below the water. The groom jumped in to save her and drowned as well. (There is no documented proof that anyone ever drowned in Ghost Lake.)

I first came to investigate Shades of Death Road with a group of NJGHS members back in the summer of 2000. It was a perfect night, not too hot, not too cool, and not too humid. The

Ghost Lake

sky was clear, and there were so many stars compared to Union County, our home base.

After traveling out Route 22 West and then up Route 31 North, we were on the county roads leading to Shades of Death Road, which is off of CR 611/Hope Road. The sun was setting as we pulled onto Shades. We wound our way over the road, going slowly to maintain the caravan of investigators and to look and listen for anything out of the ordinary. Finally, we arrived at Ghost Lake, and one by one we pulled into the gravel and dirt parking lot.

As we got out of our cars, we gathered to go over the investigative protocols and test our equipment and load fresh batteries. By now it was completely dark. Since we weren't familiar with the place, I did not allow the team members to go up the trail to look for the caves or the abandoned cabin in the woods. The group split into three teams of two investigators each and fanned out around the lake and parking area.

I was tracking the temperature with my thermal scanner while monitoring the other team members. My concern for my team members' safety went beyond the paranormal. I was worried about bears, as the area is known for its black bear population. I continued working my way from one group to the next measuring the temperature and activating the audio recorder for EVPs.

I made my way over to the entrance of the parking lot. Joe was filming with his new Sony NightShot camcorder. He took a break to show me what he had captured thus far on his digital still camera. There were a couple of decent orb pictures. He then resumed filming. I was standing next to him and scanning the temperature in the area. It was averaging around seventy-five degrees. Suddenly the temperature began to drop on the digital readout of the thermal scanner. Before I could announce this, Joe exclaimed, "I just got one! Did you see that? It just went right past the lens!"

I couldn't believe how fast the temperature dived twenty degrees. I showed Joe the readout of the scanner and how it was displaying a temperature of fifty-five degrees. As he began to rewind the video to the beginning of the orb flying by, I watched the thermal scanner register the climb in temperature back to seventy-five degrees. Joe showed me the footage, and sure enough, there was an orb that zoomed across the bushes and brush in front of us. He then slowed the playback speed so we could see the orb moving in slow motion. It was truly amazing. Not only did he have it on video, but I had the temperature drop documented to further support the event.

Other team members gathered around Joe as he showed the footage again. We were so excited we didn't notice the patrol car that had pulled into the parking lot. The officer got out of the car and asked us for identification. I explained to him that my ID was in my car and asked him if I could retrieve it. Meanwhile, other team members began explaining to him that we weren't looking to get into trouble: we were simply ghost hunting.

I knew they meant well, but my heart sank when they started telling the officer about the ghost hunting. All I could think was "Here we go. He's going to write us off as psychos." I returned with my identification and explained to him about the NJGHS. Fortunately, he was receptive. It turned out that he was a Conservation Officer and was on duty to patrol the area. He said they had a lot of problems with teenagers going up to the lake to party in the cabin in the woods. When he saw the flashing lights of our cameras, he pulled in expecting to find a rowdy bunch of drunken teens.

Joe stepped forward and showed the officer the video of the orb he just captured. This actually fascinated the officer. I explained to him the temperature drop I had at the same time the orb occurred. The officer gave me his business card and asked that if we were to come up there again to investigate, that we call him first to let him know. He said that technically we were in violation of being in the park after dusk, but he would make an exception since we weren't damaging the property and were cooperative with him.

I have been back up to Shades of Death Road several times since moving to this area. My second husband and I had a hearse named "Morticia," a 1989 Eureka high top, and I revived the Morbid Mobile Tours to employ it for the original tour in Union County and this new one in Warren County. We had a special midnight tour on Shades of Death Road on Halloween in 2005.

At 11:45 p.m., we picked up a group of tourists at the Hackettstown train station and proceeded to Shades of Death Road. The six tourists were having a great time in the back of the hearse. "Urnie," our medical-issue skeleton and mascot, sat up front between Steve, who was driving, and me. I narrated the history of the road over the radio while heading toward Ghost Lake. Once we the lake was in view, I told the legends and truth about the man-made lake.

Steve noticed police cars in the lot by the lake, but figured we were fine as we were not stopping or pulling in. We continued to the end of the road and made a U-turn to come back once more on Shades of Death. As we passed the parking lot of Ghost Lake, Steve noticed the cop cars exit the lot and begin to follow us. Sure enough, their lights came on and we had to pull over. By the time the officer reached Steve's window, I had the insurance card, registration card, and brochure of our tours to hand him. Steve handed the officer the credentials and explained that we were just driving down the street as part of our Halloween Midnight Tour. The officer pointed his flashlight to the back of the hearse, and saw the people sitting there. I think it scared him. He took a step back and said, "Oh, you're on a tour now? You've got people back there?" We assured him that they were there because they wanted to be. He laughed and yelled to his partner in the other squad car, "They're on a tour! They got people in the back of this thing!"

The officer, thankfully, had a sense of humor and explained he was relieved. He said he and his partner were not thrilled at having to pull over an older hearse at midnight on Halloween on Shades of Death Road. He kept the brochure and let us go on our way to complete the tour, which we did by cruising through the Union Cemetery in Hackettstown looking for the ghost of Tillie.

Even though you now know that the ghostly apparitions are either legend or natural atmospheric conditions, it's still worth a ride on Shades of Death Road. I would suggest driving it in the daytime to get familiar with the bends and turns of the road. There are no streetlights save for those at either end of the road. It is possible to crash into a boulder if you're not paying attention or going too quickly. Haunted motoring!

CHAPTER 9

You're a Good Ghost, Charlie Brown

HACKETTSTOWN

CHARLIE BROWN'S STEAKHOUSE RESTAURANT is on Grand Avenue in Hackettstown. The restaurant chain, indigenous to New Jersey, New York, and Pennsylvania, has a unique talent for tailoring its restaurants for existing structures rather than leveling them and rebuilding new cookie-cutter restaurants. This Charlie Brown's building dates back to 1878 as the Clarendon House.

The Clarendon saw reincarnations as a hotel, eatery, pool hall, and brothel. From 1926 to 1947, it was known as The Hackettstown Inn. In 1947, Willie and Ernie Putz, brothers from Germany, purchased and restored the ailing Clarendon building. They added another dining room to the structure in 1956. While Ernie was vacationing in Germany, his brother had a stained glass window made for the bar to face Grand Avenue. In the center of the window is a portrait of Ernie.

Under the Putz brothers' ownership, the Clarendon was the place to be in Warren County at the end of the work day. Councilmen, school board officials, and prominent citizens all convened here. It was the television show *Cheers* come to life, complete with Elwood Smith, a.k.a. "Smitty" the bartender, and Lou Morgan the flower farmer. Smitty often got into arguments with the Putz brothers and would be fired, only to have the regular patrons protest so strongly that he would resume his post behind the bar a few days later. Lou was a semipermanent fixture on *his* bar stool. He paid his bar bill once a year, at the conclusion of his Easter flower sales. He told his dirty jokes at the top of his lungs, often to the offense of some sweet elderly ladies who could hear him out in the dining room. Lou would be asked to leave the bar, but he would return a day or two later thanks again to the regular patrons' protests.

I first had dinner at Charlie Brown's in 2003. Some friends of mine, who own a haunted house in Hackettstown that would make any ghost hunter foam at the mouth, treated me and my fiancé to dinner. Now, I admit that when my friends suggested we walk around the corner to Charlie Brown's, I was not thrilled with the idea. Up to that point, my experiences at other Charlie Brown's in New Jersey had been very disappointing. I was in for a surprise, not only because of the redeeming qualities of the service and food at this Charlie Brown's but also because of the ghost stories I heard over dinner.

My friends told me that the first time they dined at the restaurant, they asked the waiter whether there were any ghosts, given the age of the building. Between this young waiter's recollection of his father's stories of the place and a female waiter who chimed in, my friends heard about a girl ghost from the brothel days. The story they heard and relayed to me was that the young woman was pregnant and the father of her unborn baby wanted nothing to do with her or the baby. She was so distraught that she drew a hot bath to relax and brought along a bottle of "comfort" for the soak. Apparently she drank too much, fell asleep, and drowned.

My friends also told me about the ghost of a little boy who has supposedly been spotted or felt in the basement by some of the restaurant staff. Needless to say, dinner was a success from where I sat at the table. I had a good meal, great friends, and talk of ghosts. My next mission was to figure out a way to conduct a paranormal investigation there.

In 2006, I was preparing for the NJ Ghost Conference to be held in Hackettstown. After securing permission from the corporate offices of Charlie Brown's, the general manager of the Hackettstown restaurant accepted my reservation for a buffet dinner and the chance to investigate the second and third floors. (This was a fringe benefit for conference attendees.) We rented the second-floor banquet room for our dinner with author Rosemary Ellen Guiley, Ph.D., and afterward, the tables were cleared away and we were allowed to mill around in the dining room with the lights down to investigate. Small groups of people took turns going up to the third floor with one of the wait staff.

The third floor is not renovated and can be a bit hazardous to negotiate, especially in the dark. Sherry Irish, team leader for the Central Jersey division of the NJGHS, and I went up to the third floor near the end of the evening with Ryan, a waiter. It's still set up the same as it was in its hotel days. I passed by the little guest rooms, some with a sink on the wall and others with a toilet fixture attached in a conspicuous place as some of the walls were missing or had gaping holes in them. The hallway, with its creaking floor boards and broken pieces of wall scattered around, would be the envy of any Halloween haunted-house attraction. Sherry and I took some pictures but discounted most of the orbs we captured since there was so much dust. Many people had been up there before us that evening and stirred up even more.

I saw a bathtub in one of the rooms and asked Ryan if that was where the young girl supposedly drowned. "No," he said, "that's actually on the second floor, but our busboys live there and are very superstitious. So we told them that it was this bathtub to put their minds at ease." (Note to readers: Please keep this information to yourself if you're dining at Charlie Brown's in Hackettstown. Good help is hard to find, and I don't want to scare off the great staff on board at this place.)

Ryan took Sherry and me up to the cupola. It is quite narrow, so only one of us could be on the ladder at a time to take in the view of the town from up there. I was more sickened by the dead bird tucked in the corner of this belfry and more scared by the threat of spiders, given all of the webs around me, than I was of a ghost.

Sadly, I did not capture anything in the way of worthy paranormal evidence this particular evening. I write it off to the fact that it had been a long day for me, given the preparation and execution of the NJ Ghost Conference. There were too many people investigating, and the restaurant downstairs was open for business, creating more noise and distraction.

In January 2007, I was filming with the television crew from the Treasure HD show *Magnificent Obsessions*. We had completed our on-site investigation the month before at Eastern State Penitentiary in Philadelphia. Now the crew came to film me at home for the background footage and to show the ghost-hunting equipment used on an investigation. When it was time to break for lunch, the producer wanted to know where we could all go to eat that would be close by and have quick service. Naturally, I suggested Charlie Brown's. On the drive over, I mentioned to them that the restaurant was haunted.

We walked in the front door as Giovanni Passione, the general manager, was walking towards the hostess station. He and I made eye contact, and before I could say, "Hello," he said, "I'm glad you're here. I had an experience this morning. I need to tell you about." In my head I was thinking, "You couldn't have timed this better, Giovanni!" He grabbed the menus and led us to the library dining room. He said that he would not seat anyone else in this room so that we could have the privacy for our lunch.

Once our waiter was off to the kitchen with our lunch orders, Giovanni proceeded to tell us what happened that morning. He said he had arrived earlier than usual, around 6:30. He went down to the basement to take inventory. He heard someone walking with heavy, deliberate footsteps around the salad bar station above him. He knew the busboys who live on the second floor use the back staircase, which leads directly to the kitchen. He also knew that if one of them had come down that staircase, he would have heard the steps creaking. Giovanni worried that perhaps he hadn't locked the front door after his arrival and someone had walked in. He crept up the basement stairs to the kitchen, grabbed the largest butcher knife he could find and went out to the dining room to see who was there. He saw no one at the salad bar. He carefully inspected both dining rooms and found them empty. "It was the first time since I've been here that I was so scared I made my way to the front door and went outside," he said. He went on to say that he remained outside until one of his office assistants arrived for work. He simply did not want to go back in the building alone.

Up to this point, any time I had seen Giovanni at Charlie Brown's, he recognized me and was pleasant, but I always sensed that he viewed me as "the crazy ghost lady." Something told me that, going forward, I would cease to be the crazy ghost lady in his eyes.

One morning in April 2008, I met with Giovanni in his office to discuss the haunting of the restaurant for this book. Giovanni had been working at the Hackettstown Charlie Brown's since it had opened in 2000. I mentioned to him the story I had heard about the young pregnant woman who drowned in the tub. He said there were different versions. One story said the young woman was a "working girl" back when there was a brothel in the building. She drew a bath for her son and went to service a client in the next room. This was multitasking at its morbid best because the son drowned in the tub. The other story said that the boy was left alone to bathe while his parents were downstairs at the bar drinking, and he drowned.

This might explain the ghost of the little boy often seen in the restaurant.

Giovanni said that he had heard there used to be an oak tree in front of the hotel and that one morning a man was discovered hanging from it. Also, one of the "ladies of the evening" from the brothel days was murdered here.

Giovanni then told me about the time a woman came into the restaurant and asked if she could just look around, even upstairs. He saw no harm in this and let her wander around. She came up to him afterwards and said that when she was about ten or eleven years old, her family had lived on the second floor and operated the business as an inn. One night she got up and went down to the kitchen to get some ice cream. Coming out of the kitchen with her ice cream, she entered the dance floor area, which today is the smaller dining room next to the bar. She saw a little girl standing in the middle of the dance floor holding a doll. She spoke to the little girl as she approached her, but the little girl did not respond. The woman said that as she got closer, a bright light appeared, and the little girl was gone. Of course, she let out a scream and woke her parents as she rushed upstairs to tell them what had just happened. They did not believe her. A few weeks later, one of her parents saw this little girl and then of course accepted the daughter's story as truth.

Giovanni also told me about a customer and his son who dine at the restaurant every so often. Up until the mid-1990s, they ran the pool hall out of what is now the banquet room on Charlie Brown's second floor. The son told Giovanni that one night he was closing up and had placed all the cues in the racks on the walls. He also racked all the balls in the triangles on each of the pool tables. The next morning when he arrived, the cues were all over the floor and the balls were scattered all over the pool tables as if someone had been playing pool all night. He called his father to see if he had stopped in with his friends, but the father said he had not been to the pool hall for the last couple days. They both felt something weird had happened, but they didn't talk about it.

I'm sure everyone has had that unmistakable and unnerving feeling of not being alone at one time or another. Giovanni had it when he was closing up one night. He went upstairs to the banquet room to make sure the lights were off. He felt like someone followed him from the kitchen to the banquet room, but he knew he was the only one there. As he entered the room, the feeling of someone behind him was so strong that he turned around expecting to see someone there. He saw no one and yet felt pressure on his shoulders as if he were carrying a young child on them. He said he was so scared that he made a hasty exit and left for the night.

A couple of times, he's also had the classic experience of seeing what he felt was a ghost out of the corner of his eye early in the morning while doing paperwork at his desk. He described to me glimpsing someone standing in the office doorway from his peripheral vision. When he would lift his head to look directly at the door, he could see a blur as if someone had just ducked out of sight. He would get up and inspect the hall to find no one there.

I asked Giovanni if any of his staff had encountered ghosts. He told me that his assistant had called him at home one morning, upset. Behind the bar, she saw a disturbing sight. Liquor bottles are usually stacked on steps behind the bar. She said that the second row of bottles was scattered all over the floor while the first row was still neatly in place. It was as if someone had taken the second row of bottles and gently laid them down on the floor in front of the first row. None of the bottles was broken. Giovanni knew that everything had been in order the night before since he had locked up, and the news upset him as well.

The last experience of Giovanni's that I'll relate is probably the most chilling. He is in the protective habit of locking his office whenever he goes downstairs. True to form, he did just that one night as he was preparing to close and went down to the bar to cash out the till. As the bartender finished cleaning the bar and Giovanni counted the cash, the bar phone rang. Giovanni could tell by the ring pattern that it was an internal phone call and figured it was someone in the kitchen, but when he looked at the phone display, he was shocked. The bartender noticed that his face was completely void of color and asked him what was wrong. "This call," he said, "is coming from my office. I locked my office before I came down here." Giovanni mustered the nerve to answer the phone. No one was on the other end. He hung up the phone, locked up the till and told the bartender, "That's it! We're done for tonight. Let's get out of here!"

The day's specials are posted on the blackboard at Charlie Brown's. As for the ghosts, they come à la carte.

CHAPTER 10

Washington Theatre
WASHINGTON

IN APRIL 2006 I HAD THE PLEASURE of investigating this historic theater in Washington (Warren County) as part of the kickoff for the NJ Ghost Conference. This event was coordinated with the theater owner, Marco Matteo.

I first met Marco, a thin young man with dark hair and glasses, when he came to my "Ghost Hunting 101" presentation at the Phillipsburg Library back in 2005. He waited outside the library for me afterward and introduced himself. Marco told me that he was leasing the old movie theater in Washington. He practically grew up there and was excited by the prospect of operating the theater and ultimately returning it to its original grandeur as a single theater with live acts on the stage. He asked me if I thought it would be haunted given how old it is. I told him I would have to investigate it to know for sure but that the odds of a residual haunting or possibly a ghost were increased given the age and "traffic" the theater had.

The Friday-Night Kickoff Investigation was humid. I could tell the April showers were on their way for our conference the next day. Since the air inside the theater was temperature controlled, we were able to take photos. It goes against NJGHS protocol to take photos in high-moisture conditions because the condensation on the camera lens can appear as orbs. I gathered the crowd of investigators around to review the investigative protocols. For most of the attendees, this was the first ghost hunt they'd ever been on. I wanted to make sure they understood about taking pictures and "calling the shot" especially if using a flash and an autofocus camera. Autofocus cameras send out an infrared beam to the subject of the photo and relay the information back to the camera to calculate the distance and amount of flash needed. When investigators are using autofocus cameras, they need to announce their turn at taking the picture so the others wait before taking their pictures. Therefore I train investigators to "call the shot" before taking their picture so that they avoid the false-positive infrared beam orb that appears when you take a photo of someone else's autofocus beam.

Kelly Weaver, psychic medium and head of the Spirit Society of Pennsylvania, came with her husband, John. Kelly has been contacted for numerous ghost investigations and has been featured on the Discovery Channel's show *A Haunting*. Kelly told me that she especially likes to investigate old theaters. This was the first time I had met Kelly. She's a bright, attractive woman with a great sense of humor. She's extremely psychic and yet down to earth.

Once I concluded the protocol review, Marco related the history of the theater. Today it houses two movie screens, but it was originally one huge theater complete with a stage for live productions and vaudeville acts. Marco had just reopened the theater after completing the leasing process and restoration.

The Washington Theater was first opened on January 24, 1927, by the St. Cloud Amusement Corporation, with John Howell and his wife, Clara, as the operators. George Miller was the projectionist, and his presence has been felt at times in the projection booth. John Howell is referred to as "Howard" by current employees. The theater had Gene Autry perform on the stage, and possibly Lou Costello since he was from Paterson. In 1978, the theater was renovated to create twin theaters, the same setup it has today. When the house lights are up, one can tell that the original orchestra pit for live stage performances has been covered up.

Once Marco completed his historical review of the theater, it was down to the ghost hunting basics. As investigators, we wanted to know what paranormal experiences Marco had had since being back in the old theater. Marco took a deep breath and began to describe his encounters. About a month before reopening the theater, during a thunderstorm, Marco was talking with his friend Dennis upstairs and noticed a glow in the stairwell. Marco said that as fast as the orb appeared, it vanished: "In the blink of an eye, it was gone."

He went on. "We went down the hall and continued to work on the sink. We were standing about four or five feet apart from one another and talking. All of a sudden, we witnessed [a] mist that came out of the wall of the hallway, traveled past us, and went directly into the other side of the hallway wall. It was a definite stream of white light or mist, almost like the tail of a kite."

That was enough right there for the seasoned and new ghost hunters to work with. We split into small groups to cover the theater. Some people went upstairs to the projection room, the offices, and of course the hallway where Marco witnessed the mist that came from the wall. Other investigators went to the stage area behind the screens or below the stage to the old dressing room areas.

I went backstage with several investigators and Kelly Weaver. As I was making my way up the tight winding staircase to the stage, I bumped my left leg on the edge of the next step I was to climb. Normally I wouldn't have even noticed. However, this part of my leg above the ankle was freshly tattooed and still very tender. Needless to say, that little bump felt like a hard smack from a leather belt. The "ouch" that I let out was heard by the gentleman behind me, who turned out to be highly sympathetic given the number of tattoos he had on his arms. He was a fireman for a nearby town and on his off days helped Marco with renovations at the theater. I cannot remember his name, but I do recall his telling me, in addition to his pain-filled tattoo stories, that he never felt alone when working backstage even though he knew full well he was the only one back there at times. The fireman recounted how he would smell a very sweet perfume while working backstage. He said as fast as he caught a whiff of it, it would be gone. He also talked about how he would be working on the far side of the stage, hear a noise from the other side of the stage, and would figure someone was coming to check on him. A few minutes would go by, and no one would interrupt him. He said that was enough to unnerve him, and he would finish what he was working on hastily and leave for the night.

Kelly decided to take a seat in a chair and meditate a bit to see if she could tune in and discern any spirit entities in the area. The rest of us remained quiet while she did this. I took a picture in her direction as she got quiet and found nothing remarkable about the image. After a few minutes, she began to say that she saw a young, slender woman with red hair who was somewhat frantically pacing back and forth across the stage. This woman appeared to Kelly to be an actress. Kelly said that she got the feeling this actress was distressed over not getting top billing or being replaced somehow on the stage. Kelly said the actress was determined to maintain her star status. I asked Marco about her. He told me that in all his research on the theater, he did not find any old ads to identify this redheaded actress. For now, she remains a mystery.

While Kelly was describing the actress, I took some more pictures of her. In a couple of the photos, there was an orb that appeared above and to one side of her. Was this the spirit of the red-headed actress that Kelly was describing? I can't say for sure, but it certainly was an interesting manifestation. Further interesting to note was the fact that when Kelly finished with her description, I took a few more pictures and none of them had any anomalies.

Next, I went below the stage to the old dressing rooms. I didn't collect any EVPs, nor did I see any anomalies on video. The tiny, boothlike rooms were frightening to me on a claustrophobic level, but certainly not on a ghostly level. As I was getting ready to leave this area and head upstairs, I bumped into Kelly Weaver. She told me that she was getting some fascinating psychic impressions of the various actors from the days of vaudeville. She could "see" them applying their makeup and getting ready to perform on stage.

From here, I spent some time in the theaters milling around the seats and the balcony area. My "ghostometer" functions poorly compared to Kelly's, but I still can honestly say I didn't sense anything out of the norm in these areas. I made my way upstairs to inspect the hallway and projection booth.

I took several digital pictures as I made my way up the stairs but didn't capture any paranormal activity. I entered the projection booth and found several other investigators already there. One woman told me that they had just experienced a cold rush of air go by them and followed it out into the hallway. Yet, strangely, none of their temperature-measuring devices picked up any change. I had just come from that direction and didn't feel any coldness go by me, nor did I capture any photographic anomalies.

I must admit, I've had it happen on other investigations, particularly in Gettysburg, Pennsylvania, on the Civil War battlefields, where we could *feel* it getting colder, but according to the thermal scanner the temperature was constant. Therefore, I didn't want to dismiss what the ladies had experienced even though it lacked tangible evidence.

From the projection booth, I made my way down the long hallway to the rooms that were vacant. I took some pictures and scanned for the ambient temperature. Everything was as normal as could be here. There was a certain "creep factor" to the empty rooms though. It was as if I were standing in a time warp. I would look at the walls and see the cracks and age, and yet I could look out the window and see a modern-day fire truck pulling into the driveway across from the theater.

By 10:00 p.m., I gathered everyone back in the lobby and made sure they had all their equipment, and we called it a night.

On February 10, 2008, I stopped into the theater to meet with Marco. He was kind enough to iterate the history of the theater for this book. I lucked out in having his friend Kris there to interview as well. Marco told me about something that had happened to them in December 2007: "After closing, Kris Felici and I were hanging out in the theater until about 1:00 a.m. and having some beers," Marco said. "There was a loud noise backstage as if something fell. It happened again about ten minutes later. The first one didn't bother me. The second time I heard it, I jumped in my seat, but the third time, it was like a straight-up authoritative slam."

Kris chimed in. "I said the nickname for John Howell— 'Howard'—and asked if he had made that loud noise. I just got so creeped out that I had to leave."

I asked Marco if he went backstage to investigate the source of the noise. He said he did as he thought it might have been some of the heavy old iron theater chairs stored there that may have fallen over. Upon inspection, he found nothing out of order. Marco said he felt extremely uncomfortable and therefore locked up and went home for the night.

Marco has great plans for turning this theater back into the focal point of entertainment for the area. He has been booking bands to perform on Saturday afternoons to give the local youth a place to hang out and enjoy the music while being safe and mindful of the curfew. Additionally, Marco has offered classic movies like *The Rocky Horror Picture Show* complete with traditional audience participation. One has to wonder if the original *13 Ghosts* will show up on the big screen to keep the theater's supernatural residents company. If you are ever in the Washington Theater neighborhood, drop by to see a movie and take special note of that shadow out of the corner of your eye or that cold chill in the seat next to you.

CHAPTER 11

The Yellow Frame Presbyterian Church

FREDON TOWNSHIP/NEWTON

THIS CONGREGATION DATES BACK TO 1750, when it would convene in Hackettstown, approximately ten miles away from its present location. By 1763, a log cabin on Dark Moon Road, in Johnsonburg, was put into service for these churchgoers to save them the trip to Hackettstown. Since they met in a cabin, services could be held only from April through October.

The Yellow Frame Presbyterian Church moved to a larger structure that was built in 1786. It sat on one of the highest ridges in northwest New Jersey, at an elevation of 880 feet. Located at the crossroads of Shaw's Lane and the King's Highway, it was still on the Warren County side of the border. In the late 1880s, the church was falling into disrepair, and it was decided to build a Queen Anne–style church and parsonage across the street in Sussex County. The old Yellow Frame Church was leveled, leaving only the cemetery in place in Warren County. The third and final location, incorporated as such in 1884, is now in the town of Fredon in Sussex County; and its cemetery is across the street in the town of Frelinghuysen, in Warren County.

The original log cabin, which was onc and half miles southeast of the present-day location, has long since been torn down, leaving behind the Dark Moon Cemetery and a stone marker indicating where the cabin once stood. The original location was also the crossroads of County Roads 519 and 612.

Crossroads have significance in the study of the paranormal. Legends tell about striking deals with the devil at the center of a crossroads at midnight. The 1930s guitarist Robert Johnson wrote the song "Cross Road Blues" about a blues man who sells his soul to become an accomplished musician, and his contemporaries suspected that the song was autobiographical. It's also been the custom in some cultures to bury convicted criminals and suicides in the center of crossroads in an attempt to bind them and prevent them from returning from the grave to strike again.

Researching this church's paranormal history was just as confusing as explaining its bi-county location. I found little discrepancies here and there that made it arduous at best to figure out the truth. The primary story of the haunting is that a new minister to the congregation in the early nineteenth century delivered his first sermon, collapsed, and died on the spot. He was buried in the church cemetery but was later exhumed and reburied in the original, now abandoned, Dark Moon Cemetery in Johnsonburg.

Reading through the history of the ministers for Yellow Frame Church on their Web site, I did not see any mention of a minister dropping dead after his sermon. The timing of the various ministers in office on the Web site does not indicate any quick turnover.

I came across a Web site (http://www.charm.net/~edrtjd/ readgen/johnsch.htm) that allowed me to extrapolate some dates, names, and reasons for the story of the minister. Joseph Thomas, a minister and missionary, was attending a church conference in the Johnsonburg area when he died of smallpox in 1835. He was originally buried in the Yellow Frame Cemetery at Shaw's Lane and the King's Highway. However, the people of the area were frightened by the contagious nature of smallpox and wanted him removed from their cemetery. Therefore, Elder John S. Maxwell had Thomas's remains exhumed and reburied in the abandoned Dark Moon Cemetery in Johnsonburg in 1850. I admit this doesn't make complete sense. Why would they wait fifteen years before moving the infected remains if the neighbors were so concerned for their health and safety?

As for the paranormal activity, it's stated that once this minister's remains were reburied, strange phenomena began to take place at the Yellow Frame Church. People reported hearing the organ playing when there was no one in the church. It's reported that a group of parishioners got together one evening to investigate the phantom organ music. As they approached the church, the doors flew open with no one there. Next, they heard the sound of someone walking through the fallen leaves. They turned to see who it was but couldn't. All they could see was the leaves moving with each invisible step. They became scared and left.

The next day, they spoke with the minister's wife about what happened to them the night before. She said she wasn't surprised given how she's witnessed the lights in the church flicking on and off when she knows that no one is there. Issue no. 9 of *Weird N.J.* magazine says of the Yellow Frame Church, "According to a local resident, the organ player was recently dismissed because she spoke openly of seeing ghosts and hearing voices." There may be some truth to this dismissal because the issue came out in 1997, and the church's Web site lists the organist as a retired music teacher from Newton High School. He took the job in 1998. Then again, the other organ player could have simply retired and it took some time to hire a replacement. Or, to take it further, the church may not have been in a rush to replace the retiring organist given the ghostly musician on staff.

The night a friend and I went up to Yellow Frame Church was perfect, at least weather-wise. It was clear, sixty-five degrees, no humidity, still too early in the season for bugs and mosquitoes, and the constellations of stars were vivid. I brought along my digital audio recorder and digital camera. I didn't want to lug around all the equipment I have since this was an impromptu visit. (Read: I didn't secure permission here.) Granted, there weren't any "No Trespassing" signs posted, but I feel better about getting permission before investigating cemeteries nonetheless.

I placed the digital audio recorder on the front step of the church after asking whether there was anyone who wanted to tell me his name or story. I hoped to capture the ghostly organ music on this recorder. I then went across the street to the cemetery. My friend had already started taking pictures there with his digital camera. I first took a picture of the brick column at the entrance that displays the dates of this cemetery as 1786–1907.

Judging from the old photograph I saw online of the Yellow Frame Church when it sat on the Warren County side of the road, I figured the original location was to the right-hand side as I entered. My friend pointed out how there were no gravestones in this area, indicating the space was once occupied by something else. I took a picture of this space and captured three small orbs. I was impressed by how easy it was. I had just entered the cemetery and already had an orb shot.

Orbs at the Yellow Frame Presbyterian Church

We were careful to continue along the designated path through the cemetery. I remembered from my daytime visit weeks before that the ground was uneven. I didn't want to risk twisting my ankle. Plus, I didn't want to risk stirring up pollen, dust, or moisture from the grass to create false orbs in the photos.

It was amazing to me to be capturing orbs so readily, and yet not in every shot. I would take a picture with two or three orbs, but in the next picture there wouldn't be any. I always take three or four consecutive pictures in the same spot to determine whether it's an actual orb. I had the sense that this cemetery was "active." I know most ghost hunters will argue that cemeteries are void of activity because they feel the ghosts have all gone to where they were happiest in life if they remained earth-bound.

Over years of ghost hunting, I've found that cemeteries, usually the newer ones, are more active than the older ones. My theory is that some spirits may be temporarily earth-bound when they are newly deceased. For whatever reason, they are semiconnected to their remains or their former surroundings. This may be because their family members are grieving and that emotional energy is holding the loved one earth-bound.

I think that for the most part the ghost will travel back to their home or place where they were happiest while alive, but they have a sense of when someone living is at their grave. I think they show up to see who's there and why. I also think that some ghosts are completely confused about their condition. Some seem to know they're dead and can't understand what happened. Some are completely clueless and go about their business unaware that the world is changing around them and fail to recognize that no one interacts with them.

I have found the most active places to be hospitals. I get a dizzy head rush feeling when a ghost is around. The stronger the presence, the stronger the head rush I experience. I get these to the point of migraine when I visit someone in the hospital. In fact, I used to volunteer at the local hospital but had to stop because the migraines came so fast and furious every time I was there. The head rushes started when I would be delivering magazines to patients and the feeling of someone following me was so intense that I would turn around several times to see who was there. No one was there, *physically*.

I believe emotional energy is what attracts ghosts to the living. Since the ghost is non-corporeal, it "feels" things emotionally or energetically. When I investigate a cemetery, I always say a little welcome address in my head to set the energies straight that I am not there to be disruptive or disrespectful.

I honestly suspected the Yellow Frame Cemetery to be very "dead" given its age. I was pleasantly surprised at how many spirits showed up to see who I was and what I was doing there. I also felt safe there. Some cemeteries have a negative feel to them. This one carried a peaceful and positive energy.

In fact, the emotional-energy-connection theory of mine

was evident in this cemetery given the photos we took. When we took pictures of headstones and the cemetery in general, we got tiny orbs off in the distance or nothing at all. When we took pictures of each other, we found crowds of orbs following close by. In fact, my friend took a picture of me walking with my back to him. There were seven orbs around me. In the next picture I turned around and there is one orb left. The others are gone.

Before leaving, I went back to the church to collect the audio recorder. I stopped the recording and activated a new one. I walked around the front of the church from one end to the other asking for names and stories. I even tested recording in Sussex County versus across the street in Warren County.

When I got home, I plugged in my headphones to listen to the audio recordings. There was nothing significant. No organ music, no disembodied footsteps or voices were recorded. In fact, the sounds I heard while in the cemetery were not recorded either. This is strange. I know for a fact I heard the pounding bass of music. I even commented to my friend, "Do you hear that?" He said he didn't hear it, and apparently neither did the audio recorder. Twice we heard neighbors' voices outside their homes and yet these did not record.

Overall, I feel Yellow Frame Church has its spirits, holy and otherwise.

CHAPTER 12

The Changewater Murders

WASHINGTON

IN WARREN COUNTY SITS THE LITTLE TOWN of Changewater, so named because of the way the upper and lower branches of the Musconetcong River separate here. It made several attempts at industrialization, including a flouring mill, distillery, and various factories, but its notoriety doesn't stem from commercial endeavors.

May 2, 1843, started out like any other workday. Stacy Bowlby walked to work at the Frank & Strader grist mill. As he walked up a hill, he noticed a large sinkhole in the road. Drawn by his curiosity, Bowlby inspected the six-foot-deep hole. He discovered the body of a man whose head was covered in blood. Across the man's face was a large fence rail. Horrified, he ran to the closest house, that of John Parke. No one answered his frantic knocks on the door, so he proceeded to the mill. Luckily, James Petty and Peter Vanatta were already at work. Bowlby told the men what he had seen up the hill and asked them to come inspect the body to determine who it was. Vanatta went to a nearby mill to gather some more men to join in this effort. A total of eight men, including Bowlby, Vanatta, and Petty, went to the sinkhole.

Petty identified the man as John Castner. He recognized Castner's work clothes because Castner was a regular customer of the mill. Petty went to get his boss, George Franks, for help. Franks arrived and took control of the situation by sending for two attorneys and the constable. Meanwhile, the men noticed tracks leading forty-five feet from the sinkhole. It appeared as though Castner had a fatal struggle with his assailant and was dragged to the hole.

Franks insisted they go to the Parkes' house even though Bowlby told him he had gone there first and no one was home. Along with Franks were Bowlby, James Haslet, and William Prall, Esquire.

As before, no one answered their knocks at the Parke house, but the door was open, and they let themselves inside. They noticed the bed had the blankets pulled up, and a pillow was placed oddly on top. Removing the pillow revealed John B. Parke's youngest sister Maria (John Castner's wife), whose head had gashes and holes in it. The men were further sickened as they pulled down the blanket to reveal three-year-old Maria Matilda's body lying across her mother's and with the same head injuries.

The men ran upstairs to find Jesse Force, a farm hand of Castner's, still barely alive in his room. Jesse was in his bed with a severe head wound. Franks sent James Haslet to retrieve a doctor.

Franks and the remaining men went into John Parke's bedroom to find him in bed with the covers pulled up to his chin and a pillow over his head. When they removed the pillow, they saw the stomach-turning sight of his crushed skull sticking out over his ear.

Ann, George Franks's wife, arrived at the house. George ran downstairs to prevent her from seeing these horrendous sights. As he reached Ann, though, he asked her where the two young Castner boys would be. She knew they slept in a trundle bed in the room adjoining their parents' bedroom. Ann and another gentleman ran to this room in a panic. The man opened the shutters and filled the room with daylight. There they saw the two boys, Victor, age nine, and John P., age six, fast asleep. Amazingly, the two boys had slept through the murders and were unharmed.

Word of the murders was sent to the Hulshizer farm, where Sarah Parke, John Parke's sister, had spent the night at their younger sister's, Rebecca (Parke) Hulshizer. Rebecca Hulshizer and her husband, William, drove Sarah home in their wagon. Meanwhile, John Parke's nephew, Peter Parke, received news of the murders. Parke said he always figured his uncle would get robbed because it was known that he hid money in the house. Yet Parke never expected his uncle to be savagely murdered.

He stopped on the way to his uncle's farm to see whether Joe Carter, his cousin, and Henry Hummer could join him. They did not believe his news, and Carter decided to keep working the fields he was plowing. I'm not sure whether it was morbid curiosity or a chance to escape the monotony of plowing, but Hummer did go with Parke.

Carter's reluctance to leave his fields was understandable. Constable John Segreaves of Greenwich Township had foreclosure orders for Carter's debt of $61.75. If Carter couldn't pay the debt, Segreaves was to take inventory and sell off his property to recoup the money. Once Segreaves tracked down Carter in nearby Washington, Carter offered him $45 in cash with a promise to pay the balance the following week. Segreaves accepted this offer, and the debtor retained his property. However, Carter was also in other financial trouble for late payments on a thresher he had purchased. He was scheduled for foreclosure on this loan unless he could come up with security from one of three men: Jacob Davis, Esquire, Imla Drake, or George Creveling.

Parke knew Davis because Davis owned the cabinet shop across from his shoe-repair shop. As a friend of Davis's, Parke was sure that Carter would have no problem getting the security signature he needed to be granted more time to repay the loan. Davis refused to sign, however. Carter hoped to sway Creveling by making a $10.50 late payment on a foreclosure Creveling had against him. Creveling accepted the late payment but refused to sign the security.

On his way to ask Imla Drake, Carter stopped and made a $20 payment to Constable Robert Vanatta for four foreclosure executions Vanatta held against him. Then he found Drake, who declined to sign the security because he was having tough financial times as well.

Carter went back and asked Davis once more. At this point, Davis agreed but said Carter would have to come back in the morning as he was on his way to arrest another man in connection with the murders. Carter anticipated this would be a problem because he had the funerals to attend the next morning. He decided to send Hummer for the signature the next day but had yet another schedule conflict: he was supposed to be in court the morning of the funerals for more loans that were in foreclosure.

Carter asked Parke for his advice on how best to handle the scheduling conflict. Parke suggested sending a letter to the judge explaining that he couldn't appear in court due to the funerals.

Carter liked the suggestion and wrote a letter on the paper Peter handed him.

Meanwhile, news of the murders had spread rapidly throughout three counties before the day was out. At the close of the week, the town was overrun with hundreds of curious people and reporters from major papers in New York, New Jersey, and Pennsylvania.

David Parke and Abraham Castner, brothers of the murdered John Parke and John Castner, each put up $500 as a reward for the arrest and conviction of the murderer. At a time when a man worked all day to make a dollar, this was a huge sum of money. A post-mortem review of the funds in John Parke's home determined that he had more than $5,600 in cash, gold, and silver.

Adding to the drama and hysterics of the murders, the ministers presiding at the funeral were raising hellfire, claiming that one of the heirs had committed the murders in order to expedite the inheritance. In short, Warren County was in a frenzy to bring the murderer to justice. Warren County's Board of Chosen Freeholders added to the sensation by pledging $800 in reward money, bringing the total to $1,800.

To capitalize on the potential windfall, Peter Vandoren, Nelson Labar, and Jacob Davis, who had refused to sign a security for Joe Carter's debt, formed a company called the Holy Alliance, whose mission was to arrest and convict anyone they could for the Changewater murders. They agreed to split the money equally. This Holy Alliance began arresting people and dragging them before the magistrate for questioning. How out of control did the manhunt get? Edward Thompson was arrested because Mr. Smith, from neighboring Hackettstown, told the magistrate that he dreamt he saw Thompson committing the murders. Fortunately, Thompson was released.

On June 14, 1843, Joe Carter was indicted for the four murders and the one assault. The prosecutor William C. Morris badly needed this indictment, as his reputation had rapidly deteriorated in the five weeks since the murders and with no convictions.

Morris insisted on separate indictments and trials for each murder. That way, if he failed to get a conviction on one charge, he would have four more chances. Morris skewed evidence by saying the letter Carter sent to the judge explaining his inability to appear in court due to the funerals was written prior to the actual murders indicating that Carter knew the murders would take place and there would be funerals to attend the day he was to appear in court. Sadly, there was no postmark or tracking numbers to corroborate Carter's version of events. Only Peter Parke could say for sure that Carter wrote the letter after the murders happened.

Morris said in his opening statement that he would prove $15,000 had been stolen from the Parke house, a clear exaggeration. Morris also pointed out that Carter did not rush to the scene of the murders and chose to keep working. He was slanting this to show that Carter's behavior was indicative of guilt. Never mind the fact that Carter was the one who helped Peter Parke for three hours the day before the funerals cleaning and preparing the church. The evidence was circumstantial at best.

Morris further asserted that Carter had two men help him carry out the murders. Peter Parke and Henry Hummer, Carter's friend and employee, were indicted as well. The trials were absolutely abysmal. The town drunk, Jesse Tiger, and the town gossip and liar, Margaret Martines, were brought in as key witnesses for the prosecution against Peter Parke. During the course of his trial, Parke wrote his "Protest," a twenty-four-page booklet in which he maintained his innocence. He hoped the sale of this booklet would provide an income for his wife and three children after his death. "It is wholly upon their evidence that I am to lose my life. Take out their evidence, and the remainder would not even create suspicion," he wrote in "Introduction and Companion to the Protest of Peter W. Parke."

In the end, Peter Parke and Joe Carter were convicted and sentenced to hang. The hangings were the first public executions in Warren County history, taking place on August 22, 1845. To further insult these hanged men, they were buried in unhallowed ground at the crossroads of what is now Route 31 and Asbury-Anderson Road. It's believed that Parke and Carter were innocent but were convicted to save face for the prosecution as the real murderer was long gone.

Given what appears to be the erroneous execution of Parke and Carter and the gruesome murders in Changewater, it stands to reason there would be either residual energy or earth-bound spirits haunting this area. In August 2007, the NJGHS conducted an investigation of the Washington Cemetery, which straddles Cemetery Road and was called the Mansfield-Woodhouse Cemetery at the time the Castners were interred there. Dina Chirico was the team leader for this investigation.

Dina first took the team to the far end of the cemetery's lower half, where the Castners' graves are located, closer to the stone wall. As she explained the history of the murders, people began to take photos. A couple of investigators got a strange anomaly in their photos. It was a weird light that could have been a bug. Dina wasn't sure whether that was the right explanation. It was unusual that two people using different cameras both captured the same light independently. In one photo, it looks like conjoined twin orbs as they're so close together. Unfortunately, the resolution of the photo is too low and gives it a grainy appearance.

As the investigation progressed, Dina made her way to the upper part of the cemetery. She told me that she had an overwhelming feeling of being watched while in the uppermost part. She tried to dismiss it, but the sense grew to the point where she felt like she was being followed. She took pictures but did not capture anything to substantiate her feelings. She also measured the temperature, which remained constant.

I visited the cemetery in 2008 to take some daytime pictures of the Castner headstones. It's a tough terrain to navigate given the slope of the hill and the uneven footing. After taking some pictures, I decided to drive to the top of the cemetery with my kids before we left. It's quite a view. On the way out, we noticed a mausoleum with the door ajar. I couldn't resist. I pulled over, and we got out of the car to inspect the crypt. Of course, by the time we got to the entrance of the mausoleum, both boys refused to go in, claiming they didn't want to encounter any spiders. I'm not a fan of spiders either, but I had to brave it just to say I did it. I cautiously entered and took a couple of pictures. There weren't any signs of anyone resting here. It appeared to be more an abandoned storage facility.

A couple of weeks later, I went back at night by myself. Yes, it breaks the NJGHS rule of never going alone because there should be someone—*living*—with you in the event you are hurt and need help. But I was more concerned with seeing for myself if there was any paranormal activity at this cemetery. I did manage to capture some faint orbs in the area of the Castner headstones. As I walked back to my car, I turned around quickly and took a picture. I captured a single bright orb. I saw the orb on my camera's LCD screen but didn't bother to examine it any further. I had the feeling that it was time to go, as if something were insisting I had worn out my welcome.

CHAPTER 13

Ringwood Manor

RINGWOOD

LOCATED ON WHAT WAS ORIGINALLY a Lenapi Indian site, Ringwood Manor and its old iron forges sit facing Sloatsburg Road in Ringwood. Magnetite iron ore was forged at the manor and used to make a chain that stretched across the Hudson River to block British warships during the American Revolution. The iron ore was also used in the production of artillery and ammunition during that war, as well as the War of 1812 and the Civil War.

Robert Erskine, a Scotland native, arrived at Ringwood to manage the forges in 1770. He was the appointed surveyor general, produced many accurate maps of the area, and discussed strategy with George Washington.

In 1807, the Ryerson family made the first significant improvements to Ringwood Manor. By 1853, Peter Cooper, an inventor, philanthropist and industrialist, had purchased the manor with his son-in-law, Abram Hewitt, for $100,000. In addition to inventing glue, gelatin, and the Tom Thumb steam locomotive, Cooper established the Cooper Union College in New York as a free college for those who could otherwise not afford it but who demonstrated how they would best benefit from such an education.

Ringwood Manor has a total of fifty-one rooms and twenty-four fireplaces. The 226-foot-long structure also boasts 250 windows, twenty-eight bedrooms, and thirteen bathrooms. It became known as the "second White House" because of lavish twelve-course dinner parties that the Hewitts hosted in the nineteenth century.

There is a family cemetery on the 582-acre property. According to legend, a brick popped out of Robert Erskine's tomb, thus letting his spirit escape and roam the property as a blue light that has been seen following cars down the long driveway. Some claim to have seen Erskine's ghost perched on his tombstone swinging a lantern back and forth. It's also claimed that the ghost of Sarah Hewitt, Abram's wife, can be seen floating on the water of the pond that she nearly drowned in as a child when her boat capsized.

I have been to Ringwood Manor several times over the years. From Memorial Day to Labor Day, there is only a $5-per-car charge to enter this beautiful estate. The tour of the manor house is free. There are many hiking trails and a picnic area on the grounds. Sadly, at the time of this writing, New Jersey was poised to cut funding to state parks, including Ringwood Manor.

While I have never experienced any ghostly encounters

during my tours of the manor, my friend Laura Lindemann did at the tender age of ten. Laura and her family had gone to Ringwood Manor for a day trip and took the tour of the manor house. The tour guide led the group up the stairs to the second floor. Laura said the group went down the hallway to the right of the top of the stairs to see the children's room. As the group progressed back up the hallway to the landing area outside the sewing room, she stayed toward the back of the crowd. She was curious and wanted the chance to explore at her own pace.

Laura poked her head into Mrs. Hewitt's bedroom. As she looked around, she felt sudden cold air around her. As she tried to figure out where this cold air was coming from, she felt a deliberate tap on her shoulder. She turned to see who it was, expecting to find another Ringwood tour guide ushering her along to the group, but there was no one there. She said she was overcome with fear and ran to catch up to her family and the tour group. She didn't tell her family what happened as it frightened her so.

When Laura first told me this experience, I suspected it to be the ghost of Eleanor Hewitt. I had read that Hans Holzer had visited Ringwood Manor with a psychic medium, Ethel Johnson Meyers, who channeled "Miss Nellie," as the Ringwood staff refers to her. Apparently Mrs. Hewitt not only wanted Dr. Holzer to leave her property, but she expressed her dissatisfaction with the entire tour business being conducted in her home.

Mrs. Hewitt's presence is identifiable by an unaccountable cold spot, which Laura first felt, and/or the scent of flowers, either roses or lavender. She's been known to move objects and steal things from the employees.

The other suspected entity at Ringwood Manor is Jackson White, an employee there during the Civil War. He was a mixture of Caucasian, African-American, and Native American and a descendant of runaway slaves. Psychics sense his energy as that of an upstart. Staff claims to hear his footsteps in various places of the manor and find no one there upon inspection.

While on the tour with my sons, I asked our guide at the conclusion of the tour if he had had any paranormal experiences while working at Ringwood Manor. He showed me a closet door in the Grand Hall. He said on a couple of occasions he was locking up and as he was about to leave through the main entrance, he would notice this closet door would be ajar. He would close it only to find it ajar again the next morning. He demonstrated for me the amount of strength it takes to open and close this door. Once closed, we waited to see if it would pop open, but it remained closed. It didn't appear to be a structural defect that was causing the door to open on its own. Of course, the standard ghostly annoyance of lighting was recounted by our guide. He said that he finds lights on that he knows for certain he turned off at closing the night before.

Photography is strictly prohibited inside the manor. In fact, upon reviewing Ringwood's Web site, I even found the following restriction: "Scientific data recorders and other electronic equipment are not permitted to be used in the Manor House on tours, and can be confiscated at the tour guide's discretion." So there goes employing your thermal scanner, EMF meter, or digital audio recorder for EVPs.

Originally, I was told they did not allow photography inside the house because the camera's flash would fade the delicate fabrics. I was also told that for security purposes, no pictures were to be taken because they did not want someone to photograph and track the security cameras and sensors in an effort to break into the manor.

The saving grace for a ghost hunter comes in the form of . . . a form. This is also on their Web site: "Researchers can, however, obtain special permission by completing a Request to Photograph and having it approved."

In 2003, I purchased the latest technology in cell phones: a camera phone. I wanted to take pictures while at the Tony Awards in New York City. I figured the security guards at Radio City would confiscate disposable cameras. I was right. I saw several women in line ahead of me have their cameras taken away upon inspection of their clutch purses. However, my cell went undetected for its camera capability. Of course, I didn't bump into anyone famous that night to grab a picture at a whopping resolution of 640k.

However, that summer I took a tour of the manor with my fiancé. I was not in the habit of taking pictures with my cell, but it did occur to me to give it a try while on the tour. I encouraged my fiancé to keep up with the group and not call attention to the fact that I was hanging back. I waited outside Mrs. Hewitt's bedroom pretending to talk on my phone. My finger discreetly placed on the button to snap pictures, I took a picture of the sewing room and her bedroom. I went down the hall and took a picture of the children's room too. I quietly rejoined the tour group as if I had been there the whole time.

I couldn't wait to get to the car to see if I had captured anything; even an orb would have been thrilling. Sadly, all I had was blurry, postage-stamp-sized pictures.

The grounds, including the historic Ringwood cemetery, are open to the public seven days a week, except for Christmas and New Year's Day, from dawn to dusk. That makes paranormal investigating at the "witching hour" and later impossible. Well, legally impossible. It can't hurt, however, to take along a digital audio recorder or video camera and inspect the cemetery during the day for EVPs. Remember, there are remnants of the magnetite iron ore in the ground, and they seem to amplify and retain the paranormal activity at Ringwood. Make sure you examine your pictures closely for a blue light anomaly, otherwise known as Robert Erskine.

CHAPTER 14

The Hermitage

Ho-ho-kus

THE ORIGINAL STRUCTURE OF THE HERMITAGE predates the Revolutionary War. George Washington, James Monroe, the Marquis de Lafayette, Benedict Arnold, and Alexander Hamilton visited this home. The double wedding of Aaron Burr and Theodosia Prevost and her half-sister, Caty, to Joseph Browne took place here on July 2, 1782.

In 1847, Elijah Rosencrantz II hired architect William Ranlett to expand and redesign the house in a beautiful Gothic Revival style. The home remained in the Rosencrantz family up until 1970, when, at the age of eighty-five, Mary Elizabeth

Rosencrantz died and willed the property to the state of New Jersey.

Mary Elizabeth enjoyed an affluent life as a child at the Hermitage. At a time when it was considered a sign of wealth to own one porcelain doll, she had several. She loved to take her dolls for a stroll on the veranda in their carriage.

In 1917, she and Aunt Bess opened a tea room using the veranda and the adjoining parlor to generate a livelihood. Aunt Bess proved to be a marketing genius with her stories of the American Revolution, the society of the Freemasons, and the secret room that was discovered at the Hermitage that contained the body of a Hessian soldier draped in an American flag. Whether that story of the Hessian's remains is true or not, it didn't negatively affect the success of the tea room. For a business that was only open from 3:00 to 6:00 p.m. May through October, it generated $470 that first year. It grew in popularity and provided a steady flow of income until the Great Depression took hold. The tea room closed for good in 1931.

Mary Elizabeth spent her later years in hardship. In 1943, her Aunt Vinnie died, leaving her servant, an Irish immigrant named Kate Zahner, destitute. Kate moved in with Mary Elizabeth. Although offers were made to buy the five-acre manor, Mary Elizabeth refused them and continued to live in poverty. She and Kate lived in just two rooms of the manor using the woodstove for heat and cooking. In fact, there was no electricity in the home until 1969, when Social Services installed it in one room for the ailing Mary.

I first went to the Hermitage for the Friday-Night Kickoff Investigation of the NJ Ghost Conference 2005. I made arrangements with Marion Brown, a docent who worked there. Marion agreed to conduct a tour of the house for our group. She supervised as we investigated both inside and outside the home.

Around 6:00 p.m., the conference attendees who were going

to participate in the investigation gathered in the hotel lobby. I reviewed the protocols for investigating while they signed in on the waiver sheet. Everyone cooperated with creating car pools, and our caravan departed for Ho-Ho-Kus.

We arrived on time for our overview with Marion. Since the sun was setting, she toured us around the outside of the home first. She pointed out the Freemason symbols that are above the window of the dining room, which used to be the main entrance. As we came around the other side of the house, Marion recounted the story of the full-body apparition witnessed by several people in broad daylight. The story was that back in the late 1970s or early 1980s, a group of state officials was visiting the Hermitage and reviewing the barn that was falling apart to decide whether to repair it or knock it down. While they were having their discussion, the barn door opened and a light-skinned African-American woman in a long skirt and carrying an infant in her arms walked out of the barn and went right past the group. One of the officials asked the woman what she was doing there. She did not respond, kept walking, and disappeared from the group's sight.

Marion suspects the apparition was that of Gin, a slave for Elijah Rosencrantz. She gave birth to three babies while owned by Elijah. These births are documented in the *Book of Black Births for Franklin Township, 1804–1832*. Marion pointed out that it could also have been the slave Sylva, who had a son, but she was freed and remained with the family until her death in the 1860s.

We came back around the house, and Marion told us that in the mid 1970s a caretaker lived on the property in a trailer with his wife and young children. The renovations to the Hermitage were under way, and the caretaker would often be in the house with the construction workers. He said he heard someone humming in the attic, but upon inspection no one was there. Each night as the last of the construction crew left, the caretaker would secure the large chain link fence surrounding the property. He would settle down in his trailer with his wife and children. After the children were put to bed, the caretaker and his wife would sit down for a cup of tea. They heard a knock on the trailer door, but when the caretaker answered it, no one was there. This continued each night for weeks. Every time they heard the knock, no one would be standing outside the door. One night the couple decided to set an extra cup on the table for tea. When they heard the knock on the door, they invited the invisible guest in to have tea with them. They sat down and explained to this mystery guest that they were only on site to protect the property while it was being renovated and that they meant no harm. That seemed to suffice as the knock never came again.

There are a couple "spirit suspects" who might have caused this knocking. One is Mary Elizabeth, who ran the tea room. Or possibly it was the spirit of Katie Zahner, who received final instructions from Mary Elizabeth on her deathbed to watch over the house.

We began the tour inside the Hermitage. Marion told us that in the 1970s one of the directors of the Hermitage entered the house one afternoon and saw a sheer black piece of fabric floating up the stairs. She pointed out the portrait of "Killie," who died at thirty-four of tuberculosis and left four small children behind. Many people report a sensation of coldness when standing near this portrait.

Marion had her own chilling experience in the back parlor, the old tea room. She said one afternoon she was closing up the house and had finished turning off the lights in the rooms upstairs and in the parlors. She was on her way out through the dining room when she heard a loud crash in the back parlor. She went to the room to find a chair had fallen over and all the lights were back on.

As we made our way upstairs, Marion noted that nothing paranormal had ever been witnessed in the "pink room." She brought us to Aunt Bess's room and said that over the past twenty years, people have heard something being dragged across the floor in the attic above this room. People describe it as the sound of a large box or trunk being dragged.

As we entered the master bedroom, Marion said that this was the most active room on the second floor. Both Killie and Mary Warner Rosencrantz, Mary Elizabeth's mother, died in this room. She pointed out the cradle and said that on the anniversary of the death of Mary Warner and on the death of her son, this cradle would rock back and forth by itself. Witnesses have seen the imprint of someone lying on the bed on the anniversary of Killie's death. Marion said that unseen hands have moved the handles on the desk drawers.

We continued back downstairs to the dining room. Marion said that the door to the china closet and the shutters on the windows have been known to open and close on their own. Toward the front of the house was the office. Many people reported hearing piano music coming from this room, and yet there was never a piano in here. The caretaker from St. Luke's in the 1950s heard the piano so distinctly while mowing the front lawn that he went inside to inspect the source of the sound. He found no one inside, and certainly no piano.

Finally we were allowed to split into smaller groups and investigate inside and outside the home. Brian Sandt and I went back down to the back parlor/former tea room. While we were passing through this room on the tour, Brian's EMF meter picked up a reading at the curio table that had some of the family artifacts on display.

Brian waved the EMF meter over the case, and once again it registered a reading indicative of an electrical source. We looked under this table to make sure there were no batteries attached to it or any electrical outlets in the floor under it. There were no outlets anywhere near this table, and behind it was the fireplace. Brian tested running the EMF meter over an outlet and a light switch in another room and got the correct reading for those sources. He came back to this little display table, and it registered the same reading once more. He tested the other furnishings in this parlor, but nothing reacted. Only this display case seemed to have a detectable energy to it. I did some EVP recordings in case someone was trying to communicate with us. I also took some pictures of the display table. No results were recorded to coordinate with the strange EMF readings Brian had found.

We went outside to investigate. Several people showed me the digital photos on their cameras' screens. They had captured some genuine orb pictures in the area where the slave ghost was seen. One conference attendee was a self-proclaimed psychic medium who traveled the country attending UFO and ghost conventions with her boyfriend. She wanted to trance channel where there was a huge pile of grass clippings, twigs, and other debris that had been cleared from the property. This is not how the NJGHS conducts an investigation, but she came all the way from California to attend this conference, so I figured, why not? I must admit she was emanating some type of energy or drawing it to her as people were capturing a huge, bright orb that hovered above her head.

I grew bored of the orbs and quietly slipped away to the front of the house. I was taking pictures on the front lawn when I noticed that I had captured an orb near a tree. I took another picture and the orb appeared to be coming closer to me. I was fascinated and kept taking picture after picture. The orb was there, and then gone, and then reappeared. I began to scope out the property more closely to discern whether this was a reflection from something or perhaps a light banking off a car passing on the street. The street is quite a distance from where I was on the front lawn. As I was running through all possible explanations for this orb in my head, a woman, Kathleen, and her daughter approached me.

Kathleen asked whether she could show me a picture she just took. She held out her camera's LCD screen in front of me and said, "What is that?" She was pointing to a blurry blue image in the lower part of the frame. I could have been knocked over with a feather at this point. "That's a full-body apparition!" I cried. As I looked more closely, it appeared to be the apparition of a little girl in a blue dress. Kathleen and her daughter were thrilled. I don't blame them. I'd be thrilled too. Talk about beginner's luck. This was their first ever ghost hunt and ghost conference. As a point of reference, I've been ghost hunting officially since 1993 and have yet to capture a full-body apparition.

I asked them to follow me to the back of the house to gather the rest of the group. It was close to our agreed time of departure, and I wanted the other investigators to see this remarkable photo. Everyone was amazed.

After the conference, Kathleen sent the picture to me for posting on the NJGHS Web site. I went online to the history section of the Hermitage's Web site. There I found a picture of young Mary Elizabeth Rosencrantz on the front lawn with her Aunt Bess. When I compared the picture on the Web site to the one Kathleen had taken, there appeared to be about ten or twenty feet between where the apparition was photographed and where young Mary Elizabeth and Aunt Bess were seated in the archived photo.

Marion thinks Kathleen captured a full-body apparition of Aunt Bess as a little girl. Aunt Bess grew up at the Hermitage and loved it so much that she bought out her brothers in order to keep it in the family. I think the apparition is Mary Warner Rosencrantz. Her portrait as young girl in the Hermitage depicts her wearing a blue dress and having long hair with banana curls. Mary Elizabeth is always pictured with very short, cropped hair. I know that Mary Warner only came to the Hermitage as an adult, but perhaps because her childhood portrait is there, she appeared in the image she felt more people would recognize.

The Hermitage proved to be a perfect venue for the Friday-Night Kickoff Investigation. It's a beautiful structure, the grounds are easy to navigate, and a member of the NJGHS got her first full-body apparition. If you want to take a Sunday drive, visit the Hermitage. Take the tour. Maybe out of the corner of your eye, you'll see a little girl in a blue dress pushing her doll carriage on the veranda.

CHAPTER 15

The Ghost of Centenary College
HACKETTSTOWN

AS ONE APPROACHES HACKETTSTOWN while
winding down the mountain on Route 46, the gleaming dome
of Centenary College comes into view. The college dates back to
1867 when it was founded as a coeducational preparatory school
by the Newark Conference of the United Methodist Church. It
is located at 400 Jefferson Street in the heart of the historic Victorian section of town.

Most students lament that there is not much to do in Hackettstown. True. It's not New York City, and the lack of nightlife
is obvious. That's not necessarily true, however, if you're one

drawn to the nightlife of the afterlife. Centenary has one of the most famous ghosts in town because it was witness to one of the most infamous crimes in town.

On April 8, 1886, Matilda "Tillie" Smith was excited about the band that was to perform in town that night. Tillie, 18 years old, was an independent young woman. She worked in the kitchen at Centenary. She also roomed at the college. Her parents lived not far away in the town of Waterloo.

Centenary had a strict curfew of 10:00 p.m. for all the females, students and employees alike. Tillie knew the band she wanted to hear would be playing past this curfew. Rather than jeopardize her job by walking into the dorm after curfew or risk missing the band's performance, she decided to ask twenty-nine-year-old James Titus, the maintenance man of the college, for help. Tillie requested that he leave a window open for her to crawl through upon her return to Centenary later that night. James was reportedly not happy with this idea but agreed to help her.

That night Tillie went downtown with the two Rice sisters and their male friend. After the performance, they walked up Main Street to Church Street. The sisters and their friend continued up Main Street while Tillie walked up Church Street to the college. Tillie never made it back that night. The next morning, April 9, her body was found in a field southwest of the college by a corner fence. Police determined that she had not been assaulted in the field because her clothing was dusty, not muddy like the area where she was discovered.

She had a severe wound to her forehead and finger marks on her throat. Conclusions were made that she was attacked and killed by more than one person. It appeared as though her clothing had been removed and replaced as one arm was half out of the sleeve of the jacket. Apparently she struggled so violently to fend off the attempted rape that her attackers, instead of quieting her, ended up strangling her to death.

People suspected two peddlers who had been in town the previous couple of days to be the murderers. One suspect was captured in Washington. He had been registered as H. Hunter from Port Jervis, New York, but the name he gave upon his capture was H. A. Baring. His partner, Charles Munich of Stroudsburg, Pennsylvania, was not caught.

The peddler was eventually released, and public outcry intensified to find the murderer. On April 28, James Titus was formally charged for the attempted rape and murder of Tillie Smith. His trial began on September 28 at the county courthouse in Belvidere. A month later, notwithstanding that most of the evidence against him was circumstantial, Titus was sentenced to hang for Tillie's murder. His appeal for a new trial was denied.

What's odd is that Titus signed a confession months after the conviction stating that he killed Tillie accidentally. This saved him from the gallows, but he spent the next nineteen years in prison. He was released on December 27, 1904, when his sentence was commuted. He returned to his home in Hackettstown and lived there for the next fifty years always asserting his innocence of the crime. He died in 1952 at the age of ninety-five and was buried in Union Cemetery in town.

Tillie was originally buried in a pauper's grave. However, on November 24, 1887, a beautiful stone-carved monument was erected in her memory from all the donations that poured in as she was seen as a symbol of feminine virtue. In fact, the inscription on the monument reads, "In defence of her honor." Yes, they spelled "defence" that way. When I took my sons to see the monument, my older son noted aloud, "Mom, they spelled 'defense' wrong." And I couldn't resist busting his chops by replying with, "No, de-fence is the thing that goes around de-yard."

Over the years, motorists have seen Tillie's ghost at the archway entrance of Union Cemetery on Mountain Avenue. Others have reported seeing her ghostly image strolling on the grounds of Centenary College. Dorm residents have reported lights flickering on the third floor of the south dormitory where she resided when she worked at Centenary.

Other traditions have risen as a result of Tillie's ghostly presence. Female dorm residents leave flowers or little trinkets outside their doors at the start of the semester to appease the ghost of Tillie to watch over and protect them while at school. If one visits Tillie's monument in May, around commencement time, there will be flowers tucked into the arm of the female figure carved from the stone. It's the female graduating students' way of saying thanks for the protection they felt while attending Centenary.

The best personal account I can give for the ghost of Tillie comes from my friend Peter who lives here in town—very close to Church Street, in fact. Peter and I worked together at the same company, in the same department. Still, work being as hectic as it was, we rarely got time to talk. Once in a while I would make my way over to his cubicle and visit. Sometimes he made it down to my end of the floor to chat.

One morning I didn't have the patience for the elevator to arrive at the lobby, so I took the stairs to the third floor. I rarely took the stairs and therefore rarely passed Peter's cubicle on the way to mine. As I walked by, Peter motioned to me and said, "L'Aura, I need to talk to you." I turned and said, "Okay, let me put my stuff down and I'll come back." (When I say "stuff," I mean I was a pack mule. I had my purse, laptop/briefcase, and gym bag with all my herbs, dietary supplements, lunch, and workout clothes packed.) I quickly threw the computer into the docking station, stashed my purse in my locker, and crammed my gym bag under my desk.

I went back to see Peter at his cubicle. "You're not going to believe this," he told me, "but I think I saw the ghost of Tillie this morning." I sat on the edge of his desk and said, "Of course

I'd believe you. Tell me what happened."

Peter said that he had decided to start a new health regimen to lose ten or twenty pounds (the equivalent, for a male, of skipping a Big Mac twice a week), especially since warmer weather was approaching. His plan was to get up an hour earlier for work and go for a walk and on alternating mornings going to the gym to work out. This particular morning was the "go for a walk" morning. He was out the door a little after 5:00 a.m. I don't remember the exact route he took, but it was long. It was dark when he started out, but by the time he neared the end of his walk, he was getting close to Centenary College. He came up Jefferson Street and was going to turn down Church Street to head home. As he approached the college, the sun was barely cresting the horizon, and the available daylight was enough to make out a figure of someone walking on the front lawn of the campus closer to the corner of Moore Street. He said he thought nothing of it. He figured another person was out for an early-morning walk, or maybe a co-ed was returning home to the dorms from the night before.

As he got closer to the main gate of the college, his eyes focused on the figure, and he realized she was dressed in Victorian clothing. She had on a long, dark-brown or black skirt and a short jacket. Peter stopped in his tracks and watched the woman continue walking toward the building and then vanished from sight. He ran to the spot where he saw her last to look for any signs a person had been there, like footprints. He didn't see any marks on the soft dewy grass. He realized it had to have been the ghost of Tillie. He bolted home to get showered and dressed and made his way into work to tell me about the experience.

I asked him to keep me posted if he saw her again. He agreed but never caught a glimpse of her again. This could be because work demands increased to suffocating proportions for Peter and he wasn't going out for early-morning walks as planned.

For a short while, I was heading out the door at 4:00 a.m. to run down to the Quick Check on Mountain Avenue, across from Union Cemetery, and back home to complete two miles. Initially it was all I could do to make it in forty-five minutes, but I cut that down to twenty-five minutes.

One morning while making the run, I was heading down Washington Avenue. Since it was still dark, I could see the hint of headlights approaching Washington from West Plane Street. I knew to slow my pace to let this car cross the intersection. The car was slowing to the stop sign, and I realized it was a Hackettstown police car. The officer driving the car didn't have forewarning of my presence the way I did with his car's headlights. I stopped just before the intersection so he could cross. He saw me right as he got to the intersection and slammed on his brakes. He looked startled. Apparently he was not expecting to see someone coming down the street at that ungodly hour. I waved to him, and he seemed to snap out of his shock. He then turned to face forward once more and drove on.

I was careful not to jog near Centenary. I know it sounds contradictory that a ghost hunter would avoid the opportunity to witness a full-body apparition, but there's a time and place for everything. I would kick myself if I saw Tillie while running because I wouldn't have my camera with me. The saying "ignorance is bliss" applies here. I'd rather not know and avoid the college than see her and not be able to document her with a photo.

The NJGHS has investigated the Union Cemetery on several occasions. Nothing has ever been detected there in terms of EVPs or orb shots. For all intents and purposes, it's dead. Yet we convened one cemetery hunt behind the community center on Main Street so we could document the Presbyterian Church cemetery—the oldest in town, dating back to 1763. Many of the headstones are broken or have fallen down. And of course on the night we showed up to investigate, the local marching band was practicing in the community center's parking lot. So there went our chances of collecting EVPs. However, several of us managed to capture some valid orb pictures in this tiny cemetery. It's amazing to think how the Union Cemetery appeared to be the perfect place to ghost hunt given how large and removed from traffic and noise it is, and yet we fared better that evening in the Presbyterian cemetery, which is the size of a 7-Eleven convenience store.

Even though I have not yet encountered the ghost of Tillie, I sense that she has a rich "spiritual life" given what other people have seen and the traditions of the students of Centenary College.

CHAPTER 16

The Publick House

CHESTER

THE PUBLICK HOUSE IN CHESTER is the scene of
some ghostly activity and unusual parking conditions. It was
originally called the Brick Hotel when it was built in 1810 by
Jacob Drake and son Zephaniah. This hotel served as the gathering spot in town for politics and other topics of debate. In 1867,
Chester grew overnight as a prosperous center of Morris County
because of the discovery and mining of iron ore. However, only
twenty-five years later, the iron ore was depleted and Chester
became a "ghost town."

Today the town is the quintessential country-drive destination for city residents and suburbanites. Quaint little shops,

antique stores, and even a tea room dot the landscape along Main Street.

Growing up, I remember the Publick House as one of my gram's favorite places to visit. She would have lunch with her Aunt Lydia, yes my great-great aunt, and then stroll up and down Main Street afterward to shop. I didn't get to dine at the Publick House until 2000. A friend and NJGHS member, Peter, invited me to have dinner there with him and his partner, Charles.

It was a cold winter evening when I met them. Luckily, we were seated at a table not far from the roaring fire in the fireplace. It had a comfy, Early American interior design, like a higher-end Cracker Barrel. Peter told me about the haunting aspect of the Publick House when he invited me to dinner. I suspected he was trying to entice me to dine with him and Charles. What better way than to invite a ghost hunter to a haunted restaurant? (For the record, I would dine with them at McDonald's as they are that much fun to be with, ghost or no ghost.)

Peter is gifted intuitively and can "see" spirits. I first got to know him and how his ability to see ghosts works when he participated in one of my NJGHS cemetery hunts. He told me how he could see them as shadows or like heat waves that appear coming up off the road in the summer. He also has the ability to "talk" telepathically with his mom.

After we placed our dinner order, I asked Peter what made him think the place was haunted. He said the first time that he and Charles had dinner there, they were seated at the table directly in front of the fireplace. That should have been nice and toasty, you would think. Instead, Charles had inexplicable chills and would periodically comment about how cold it was. Peter said he could see the spirit form of a little girl standing between Charles and the fire, but he knew better than to say so to Charles. Charles is a grounded, pragmatic man who, back then, did not give any credence to ghosts. Peter figured Charles chose to discount ghosts because they frightened him or made him uncomfortable.

However, Charles caught on after the fifth time he commented about how cold it was and noticed Peter staring past him. He asked Peter what he was looking at and then quickly said, "I don't want to know." But curiosity got the better of him, and he asked, "What is it? Is there something here?" To which Peter replied, "Yes, *she's* standing next to you."

There's nothing like a ghost experience for an appetizer. It's fat-free and high-energy. We did enjoy our dinner for the food as well. Afterward, we wandered around the entrance and bar areas to see if Peter could detect any ghosts. It must have been their night off as he didn't see any.

I went home and didn't think about the Publick House for several years, until I got an e-mail from Paul Viggiano. He was one of the partners purchasing the Publick House. They had contractors working on the building to renovate it, and he was handling the details to ready the place for its grand reopening. In the process of this reconstruction, he had begun to hear eerie noises and notice other odd occurrences.

I skipped my customary reply e-mail and called him at the number he provided in his message. Paul e-mailed me a couple of the pictures he had taken while we were on the phone. I saw the orb shots, and he explained how he actually saw some of these out of the corner of his eye, and he was able to capture them in a picture. I agreed that an investigation was in order.

My husband at the time, Steve, and I arrived to investigate the night of May 29. Paul warned us ahead of time that the place was under construction and there was no running water. With my postage-stamp-sized bladder, that meant no "caffing up" at Dunkin' Donuts on the way there.

Paul had his computer set up in the entrance area adjacent to the bar and in front of the door that led to the dining room where

I had had dinner years ago with Peter and Charles. We reviewed the various digital photos he had on the computer, and I took a video of this entire interview. I wish I had the pictures he took of the hallway that included apparitions of a woman, a man, a boy, and a dog. In the first picture, I could see the woman dressed in Victorian garb and a hat staring in through the left pane of glass on the door. The gentleman was visible in the right pane of glass. He appeared to be in profile view, and his hat or cap was discernable on his head. The little boy's face appeared in the lower right pane, and the dog's head appeared in the lower left. In the very next picture the apparitions were there except it appeared that the female was reaching her hand through the door. The apparitions were visible but not knock-you-over-the-head obvious. They're ghosts, not Ford models. Getting them to pose for the picture is not an easy task. Conversely, a ghost hunter's eye would discern these images as something other than a camera flaw or reflection.

The woman ghost in the photo may be Mrs. Drake. Jacob's wife was not pleased with the sale of liquor at the tavern since it was located close to many churches in town. When she died, her body was buried on the property. Today, it's under the parking lot of the Publick House.

Before we went on a tour of the place, Paul and his partner had a special surprise for me. His partner sat down at the piano and began to play. Paul sang the song "Laura Paranora" to the tune of "Georgia on My Mind." Paul admitted after his performance, which was very good, by the way, that he and his friend had drafted the song about thirty minutes before I arrived. I've had people bake me ghost-shaped cookies and give me little ghost-themed trinkets and jewelry for my presentations or investigations, but never was I so honored with my own tribute song.

We followed Paul down the hall to the door the apparitions appeared to be peering through. I was video recording in Night-

Shot mode on the Sony Handycam 201 while Steve took pictures with the Sony CyberShot digital camera and tracked the temperature with the thermal scanner. Paul pointed out where he was standing when he saw the orbs, about three of them, out of the corner of his eye. There were about a dozen in the photo.

As we passed by the kitchen, Paul said that he's seen the ghost of a young girl with pigtails in her hair there many times. I went in to film but didn't capture anything notable. I couldn't help but wonder whether this was the same spirit girl my friend Charles had standing next to him.

I asked Paul about any deaths occurring at the Publick House. He said that in its 195-year history, there had been twelve murders. I read in my research that a bartender claimed someone died by hanging in guest room 305. Unfortunately, it was too dark to see room numbers on the various guest rooms we visited.

The first room we inspected was where Paul heard a growling noise. We went on to the room where he and his partner said it always feels twenty to thirty degrees colder and they smell sweet perfume. Paul refers to this room as the "bible room." He found the bible on the dresser open to the chapter of Zephaniah—interesting given the name of Zephaniah Drakes—but I had my suspicions that someone had contrived this.

Paul explained about the bed in this room being made up perfectly only to be found hours later all disheveled. I asked if we could test it. I filmed the bed after he smoothed out the bedspread. Returning to the hallway, we all felt a cold spot, yet the thermal scanner didn't detect a drop in temperature. The ambient temperature was sixty-four degrees. We went into the "devil's room." Paul explained that he found a painting on the wall of the devil's head when he moved a bureau to ready the room to be primed and painted. He felt the former occupants were practicing Santeria. He used turpentine to remove the image.

We could still see what looked like mold in the shape of the original portrait.

We returned to the "bible room" before heading up to the third floor to check the status of the bedspread. It was still perfectly neat.

We continued to the third floor and entered the room that had a teddy bear on the bed. Paul said he originally found this bear squished in between a folded rollaway bed—not that this is paranormal, but it does make a person wonder why a stuffed bear would be left like that. It's just strange. The room was in relatively good shape and furnished nicely. I did not capture any anomalies on video there. The temperature was constant at sixty-seven degrees, and no photos revealed any orbs.

We concluded the investigation for the evening. Steve and I returned home to spend the next day reviewing the data. The best orb in motion was on video during the "Laura Paranora" song. Other than that, nothing else in the way of paranormal phenomena was captured.

The Publick House is in successful operation as a restaurant once again. Go for dinner, and bring along your camera to take a few photos while hanging out at the bar. People claim to have seen the full-body apparitions of a woman and a man walk across the floor and vanish. The descriptions of these apparitions match what I saw in the photo of the door Paul had taken. "Party of four—no wait, two: your table is ready."

CHAPTER 17

Haunted Hobart Manor

WAYNE

HOBART MANOR

LONG BEFORE I WAS A GHOST HUNTER, I attended business school to become a certified administrative assistant. While working full time, I went to class three nights a week. A fellow student and friend of mine was attending William Paterson University during the day rather than working. She figured a degree wouldn't be enough, and having the secretarial skills would be a great way to get her foot in the door to a good company.

One night after classes, my friend and I went out for drinks. This is when I first heard that Hobart Manor at William Paterson is haunted. While I thought it was interesting conversation for the evening, I was very much into my linear, "Jill Corporate" mindset and dismissed the conversation completely by the time I got home that night. I continued to get my administrative certificate and went on to a better, brighter corporate life. Here I am all these years later, paranormal investigating and writing about haunted sites in New Jersey. Who knew?

I've been to Hobart Manor in the daytime and nighttime, but the night I was there, it was so crowded with people exiting the show I went to see on campus that I didn't bother to snoop around.

The manor itself dates to 1877 when Scottish immigrant John McCullough constructed the castle complete with two turrets. By 1902, McCullough had returned to Scotland, and the castle was sold at auction to Jennie Tuttle Hobart, the widow of former Vice President Garret A. Hobart. She gave the manor to her son, Garret Jr., as a Christmas present that year. From 1915 to 1919, Garret Jr. remodeled and expanded the manor to forty rooms and moved there with his wife and children. His mother came to live with them in 1940 and passed away in January 1941. Garrett, too, passed that same year, in September.

In 1948, Caroline Frye Hobart, Garret Jr.'s widow, sold the manor to the state of New Jersey for $200,000. It then became the Paterson State Teachers College. It went through many changes to accommodate the growing university's needs, from classrooms and library to administrative offices and mailroom. By 1985, it was officially named Hobart Manor and was placed on the New Jersey and National Register of Historic Places. Restoration brought out the beauty of the manor by fixing the leaded-glass windows, refinishing the hardwood floors, and removing the partitions that had been installed over the years. The plumbing and electrical services were repaired and updated as well.

I remember the conversation with my friend vaguely. She said that the security guards on campus told her they had witnessed faces of people staring out the windows of the manor when they knew for a fact that no one was in the building.

While researching, I came across several ghost stories relating to Hobart Manor. The first involves a Sergeant MacFarlane, of campus police. He worked the midnight shift, and while on duty he went to open the basement door. He felt the door pull shut from his hand. He couldn't understand it as there was no breeze or draft to account for this force. He attempted to open it again and it slammed shut once more. The third time he pulled the door open strongly and reached inside for the pull cord to turn the light on. As soon as he pulled the cord, the light bulb shattered. He made a hasty exit.

On a separate occasion, MacFarlane was in the manor with another security officer who brought her German shepherd along. As they approached the mechanical room, the dog became anxious. His fur stood up on his back, and he grabbed his owner's sleeve to prevent her from entering the room. The legend is that a baby died in this room. Occasionally the sound of a baby crying is heard in the manor. Perhaps this particular night the baby's cries were audible only to a dog?

MacFarlane is still active on the campus police for William Paterson University and has since been promoted to captain. I think this speaks to his credibility.

MacFarlane is not alone in his Hobart Manor ghost encounter. A now-retired security officer refused to enter the manor after he saw the ghostly apparition of an old woman there. He suspected it to be the ghost of Jennie Hobart, but that did not offer him enough comfort to ever brave entering the manor again. Yet another nameless security officer experienced being pushed against the wall on the main spiral staircase by an unseen hand.

Security Officer Robert Baker saw an apparition of a man in a coachman's uniform standing in front of the manor. As Baker approached him, the man simply vanished. This ghostly fellow with his top hat, cloak, and cane was witnessed by a part-time student who was also a reporter for the local paper. She saw him while looking out the window of Raubinger Hall. To make sure she wasn't hallucinating, she tapped a fellow student next to her and motioned for her to look out the window, and she saw it too. No sooner did she have a confirming witness than the gentleman disappeared.

People have reported hearing a piano playing when in fact there is no piano in the manor. This happened during a "phone-a-thon," according to a former student. They heard the piano music coming from the third floor.

Some people feel that the ghost of Jennie Hobart is present at Hobart Manor. There are reports of seeing a woman in a long white dress making her rounds room to room as if readying the place for a social gathering.

During the renovations, an employee stopped in to pick up some paperwork. She had her three-year-old son with her. The boy became engaged in conversation with someone his mother could not see. When she asked him who he was talking to he said, "The grandma, an old lady wearing a white dress. She's standing right here." When his mother pressed him for details about the woman, such as how tall she was, he said the woman was simply floating. On later visits, the boy told his mother that the lady ghost was upset with the renovations to the house and that she would have to "go away until they are done."

In 1991, famous self-proclaimed demonologists Ed and Lorraine Warren were brought on campus to investigate Hobart Manor. Lorraine is a psychic with strong clairvoyant abilities. She detected a couple of spirits at the manor. In particular, she saw the image of a young man sitting on the main staircase reading a newspaper. This might have been the residual haunting of Garret Jr.

According to a 2005 interview with then William Paterson University President Arnold Speert, Hobart Manor is not haunted. The president for ten years at that time maintained that he had worked late on several occasions and never heard any unearthly sounds. He never saw the ghost of Jennie or her son reading the paper on the stairs. He found nothing but comedy in these ghost stories.

I've been inside the manor in broad daylight. It's a beautiful place. They've done an amazing job restoring and furnishing it. I went there hoping to interview a current employee for the book. I could hear a woman's voice coming from one of the offices. I followed the voice to a room with empty desks. I heard her voice emanating from the office at the end of this room. I could tell she was on the phone, and I didn't want to interrupt her. So I ventured into the hallway and noticed the leftover breakfast items on a skirted table. It was tempting, but I refrained. I could hear the woman was still on the phone. I figured I would buy some time waiting for her conversation to end and take a look upstairs.

Hobart Manor stairs

I climbed the staircase the security guard was pushed on. I made it safely to the top while pausing intermittently to take some photos. There is a beautiful chaise or "fainting couch" in front of the picture window on the landing of the second floor. I went into the room to the right of this window. The room is decorated in a feminine fashion with its faint yellow walls and floral detailing.

From here I turned around and went across the landing to the large living room. This handsome room was a deep burgundy color with two camelback couches facing each other in front of the fireplace. At the far end of the room was a black grand piano. I'm not sure when this piano made its debut at the manor, but any sounds of tinkling ivories can certainly be explained going forward.

Passing through this room, I found the dining room. It was a large room with seating for ten around the table. The decor was somewhat Spartan compared with what I've seen in houses of this caliber, but tasteful. I was tempted to snoop a little more, but I heard the door open downstairs. I quietly made my way to the landing and peered down as best I could without revealing too much of my presence. It appeared that whoever came in went to the office area rather than up the stairs. I went down the stairs quickly and quietly.

Once outside, I turned to face the manor to see whether Jennie was waving good-bye to me from one of the windows, or perhaps Garret Jr. was reaching for his top hat and cape to join me for a walk on the grounds. No such luck. I took a couple more pictures just to be sure.

I have to give the president of the university credit. I found the manor to be a little intimidating in the daytime. I definitely would not want to work there late at night, especially alone.

CHAPTER 18

The Halls of Morristown:
Acorn Hall and Macculloch Hall
MORRISTOWN

AMIDST ALL THE CHANGE OF MORRISTOWN, the insertion of Route 287 and the revamping of the Governor Morris Inn into a Westin hotel, sits the 1853 Italianate mansion of Acorn Hall. Its namesake, the mighty red oak tree that stood on the property for more than 200 years, is no longer there. Acorn Hall is on the New Jersey and National Register of Historic Places. Behind the house are manicured gardens and a mile-long footpath that leads to the Frelinghuysen Arboretum.

My grandmother first brought my brother and me to tour Acorn Hall in the 1970s. I think it was her way of getting her "garden fix." Plus, I think this was her attempt at getting us out of the house and breaking up the summer vacation monotony of sleep, eat, and play. I remember being fascinated by the place. Granted, I never retained the names of the owners or any other historical details relating to Acorn Hall, but I was never bored when we went there. There was something about this place that even as a child held my attention.

As an adult I went back to Acorn Hall with my two sons, ages fifteen and nine at the time, to see what their reaction would be to the place. They behaved politely, but I sensed their underlying boredom. Our tour guide was dressed in Victorian period mourning attire, all black. She did an excellent job detailing the history about the two prominent family owners of the mansion: Schermerhorn and Crane-Hone.

We started our tour in the main hallway outside of the formal front parlor and went across the hall into the library. We continued into the dining room and routed through the small hallway outside the kitchen to head up the main staircase. The furnishings and wall coverings are what make Acorn Hall unique. They are originals—no reproductions. After we finished touring the bedrooms upstairs, our tour concluded downstairs in the music room. As our tour guide took a seat at the grand piano, she asked if we had any questions about the house or the Victorian time period. Before I could formulate a question, my younger son, Trent, blurted out, "Do you have any ghosts here?"

He had the right idea to suspect the place to be haunted given how old it is. He knows I'm a ghost hunter; I just didn't think he would come right out and ask. I didn't have time to interject a "cover up" for his question. The tour guide leaned over closely to Trent and said, "People have seen her coming down the main staircase that you just came down."

As I was processing all this, my older son, Brian, volunteered, "My mom's a ghost hunter. She runs the New Jersey Ghost Hunters Society." The tour guide looked at me and smiled. I could feel the deer-in-the-headlights expression on my face. I finally mustered the strength to say, "Really, seen *her* coming down those stairs?" The guide confirmed that people have heard the crinkling noise of the dress as she descends the stairs.

I asked permission to return to the staircase to take some pictures. I tried taking pictures of the stairs themselves first and then with my boys standing on them. I wanted to see whether the spirit would react to someone on the stairs. I got a couple of pictures of my sons arguing over who would be on the step above the other, but that was about it. Nothing paranormal presented itself in the photos.

I went back to Acorn Hall in 2008 specifically for the writing of this book. I first spoke with Carie, a volunteer for the Morristown Historical Society, who said the place is mentioned in books as being haunted but that she has never witnessed any ghostly activity. Linda Lee Macken's book *Ghosts of the Garden State II* (page 36) says, "Witnesses who have seen widow Schermerhorn's ghost describe her wearing a taffeta dress, bonnet and carrying a wicker basket on her arm." I asked Carie about this ghost, and she said she has not worked at Acorn Hall as long as Karen Ann, who would be my tour guide on this visit.

Karen Ann confirmed that she has worked till all hours over the past ten years at Acorn Hall and never witnessed a ghost lady coming down the main staircase. She said that when they experience computer problems at the hall, they jokingly blame it on Mary Crane-Hone, who donated Acorn Hall to the Morristown Historical Society in 1971.

Karen Ann said that Mary was a woman of conviction and independence. She went off to Europe to study acting and returned home to live and work in New York City. She resided at Acorn Hall once it was bequeathed to her. She had many marriage proposals but never accepted any of them. Mary's spunk is best exemplified by climbing—in her 60s—on a bulldozer to protest the construction of a highway through the historic section of Morristown. Karen Ann feels that Mary would have the energy to make sure Acorn Hall is doing fine from beyond the grave.

As we concluded the tour in the gift shop, Karen Ann told me how psychics who have toured Acorn Hall usually claim to sense a spirit or energy in here. She also said that most people on the tours express a feeling of being ill at ease in the master bedroom. As for the porch swing that people claim to hear swinging on the porch, Karen Ann said there has never been such a swing at Acorn Hall. The original structure was a simple center-hall farmhouse. In 1860, the front porch, center tower, and dining room were added in the Italianate design.

I was able to take some more photos during my most recent visit to Acorn Hall, without a flash. I did not capture any paranormal anomalies. I also recorded the entire tour I had with Karen Ann on my Sony ICD-ST25 digital audio recorder. No EVPs were found upon playback at home.

I have a copper tea kettle that was given to my great-uncle Harry (Odenthal) when he was working on the restoration of Acorn Hall. He found it in the attic. He was allowed to keep it since it wasn't anything of value like the other items on display. He gave it to my grandmother, who proudly displayed it in her living room. Years later she gave it to me, and I placed it in the curio cabinet in my living room. It may be coincidence, but my life seemed to go down the drain once I put that kettle on display. I did not clue into this until my marriage was over and I packed up my belongings and moved. I noticed that life was improving, and yet every time I went through my things in storage and took the kettle out to admire it, within days something would go wrong in my life. The car would need expensive repairs, I would get very sick or some other bad news would impact my life. Just to be safe, I've left that kettle alone in storage.

I have the feeling there is more than the obvious history at

Acorn Hall. I would like to return if the staff conducts its Victorian Mourning reenactment during the Halloween season. Supposedly the veil between this life and the afterlife is thinnest at that time of year, and having a "toe pincher" coffin in the front parlor and the docents in Victorian mourning garb might improve one's chances of experiencing the ghostly aspects of Acorn Hall.

After touring Acorn Hall, I crossed Morristown to Macculloch Hall. This beautiful mansion spans 125 feet across, has twenty-six rooms, nine bedrooms, five chandeliers and a grand staircase with a black-birch railing. Macculloch Hall boasts a fine collection of eighteenth- and nineteenth-century American and English artwork and antiques as well as a vast silverware collection. Former Macculloch neighbor and artist Thomas Nast has his largest collection of artwork at Macculloch Hall.

George Macculloch immigrated to Morristown in 1806 with his wife, Louisa, and their two children. George began construction of his mansion in 1810. Having lived in London, where Louisa was a stage actress, he insisted on building his home from brick to safeguard his family against fire.

Macculloch Hall

George is most famous for his foresight in the construction of the Morris Canal. Yet I found his connection to the infamous Morristown murderer Antoine Le Blanc most relevant to this book. George's son and son-in-law were opposing attorneys for the Le Blanc trial.

Antoine was from the French West Indies. He came to the Sayre Farm in Morristown on South Street expecting to manage a huge plantation. He became disgruntled by working as nothing more than a common farm hand. He plotted the murder of Judge Samuel Sayre and his wife, Sara, by luring them separately to the barn and bludgeoning them with a shovel. He murdered their servant girl, Phoebe, in her bedroom, in order to gather the silverware and valuables to make his escape.

A posse was assembled, and Antoine was captured and brought back to Morristown for trial. He was convicted and hanged on the green in the center of town. After the hanging, his body was taken to a tannery. However, Dr. Issac Canfield and Dr. Joseph Henry first conducted experiments on the body using electrical current to see whether the muscles could be reanimated. They did manage to get Antoine's eyes to roll in the head and his mouth to grin, as well as other muscles to contract, but none caught the spark of life. Subsequent to these macabre experiments, the body was skinned and wallets were made and sold to alleviate the costs of the trial and hanging. My great-grandmother, Reta Veader, owned one of these wallets.

George Macculloch was present for the experiments and tanning of Antoine Le Blanc, which he detailed in his letters. When I met with museum director David Breslauer, he told me that George's letters detail the experiment to the point where George admits feeling nauseated. These letters are safely stored at Macculloch Hall and are not on public display.

Note to readers: All that remains of the Sayre farm is a plaque on South Street. Sadly, Commerce Bank leveled the remains of the farmhouse, which was part of the restaurant at that time, and appropriately called "Jimmy's Haunt."

Prior to meeting with David Breslauer, I interviewed the new administrator of Macculloch Hall, Jana Morgan. Jana told me about a strange experience that went on for a couple of weeks in her office. She said that she had a large button whose circumference would equal that of a baseball's. She would wedge this button into the frame of the window to the right side of her desk as she found it decorative. When she would arrive to work each morning and unlock her office, she would find the button removed from the window and on the opposite side of the office. She gave up replacing the button in the window.

According to David Breslauer, the main thoroughfare for ghostly sightings is from the foyer by the grand staircase to the music room. He said that the apparitions are so strong at times that he thought they were human until they passed through whatever table or piece of furniture was in their path.

Macculloch Hall was not just a house for the family. It was the social epicenter of Morristown's gala events. It's quite possible that the apparitions David has witnessed on occasion are the spectral remnants of the partygoers, what we paranormal investigators call a residual haunting. Yet what Jana encountered tells me that there is at least one interactive spirit at Macculloch Hall. Maybe Louisa is managing the household as she sees fit from beyond the grave. Then again, George, who died in 1858 in the master bedroom, could be exerting his control over what goes where in his home. Whatever or whoever the ghost may be, Macculloch Hall is worth the visit.

CHAPTER 19

The Bernardsville Library

BERNARDSVILLE

THE BERNARDSVILLE LIBRARY STARTED LIFE in the 1700s as the Vealtown Tavern. Captain John Parker was the owner, and his daughter, Phyllis, assisted him with the inn and tavern's day-to-day operations.

According to the story, of which there are several variations, Phyllis fell in love with the dashing Dr. Byram, a guest at the inn. Dr. Byram returned the affections of Phyllis and they were engaged.

During the Revolutionary War, General Anthony Wayne realized that certain military documents were missing. He suspected Dr. Byram, who was also missing from the Vealtown at that time. Of course, it wasn't suspicious for a doctor to be gone for a few days at a time; however, General Wayne recognized Dr. Byram as Aaron Wilde, a Tory spy. A posse was assembled to track down Wilde. He was captured at Blazure's Corner. The missing papers were found in his satchel. Wilde was convicted and hanged.

Out of respect for his daughter, Captain Parker requested the spy's body be brought back to the tavern so that he could arrange a proper burial. The body was placed in a pine box and sealed. Continental Army soldiers marched up the front steps of the tavern carrying the coffin with Wilde's body inside. They proceeded toward the back of the tavern to the kitchen and dropped the pine box on the table with a thud, turned about face, and marched out of the tavern with the door slamming shut behind them. Here is where the story tends to vary. Some say that Phyllis heard this noise while she was upstairs and came running down to the kitchen to see the coffin on the counter. She grabbed an ax or meat cleaver and hacked enough wood away to reveal her bulging-eyed, dead fiancé. She let out a horrific scream and sobbed inconsolably. The other version says that she suspected something was amiss when the soldiers would not make eye contact with her while at the tavern and would dodge her questions about Dr. Byram. She waited until nighttime to sneak into the kitchen and pry open the pine box, with the same results.

Historians argue that Phyllis Parker never existed. They say that Captain Parker's grave is documented, but there is no documentation of Phyllis's birth or death. They also say that Captain Parker would have been only fifteen years old when he fathered Phyllis, but given basic biology, this is plausible.

It's said that Phyllis went insane after discovering her dead fiancé in the kitchen. In Phyllis's time, a mental illness was a stigma on the family. The afflicted person was usually sequestered from the public. It's quite possible that Captain Parker didn't want the shame and embarrassment of his traumatized daughter to reflect negatively on him and his business. He could have locked her away in her room to live out her days and be forgotten by the rest of the world.

Whether or not Captain Parker wrote off his daughter, the paranormal record is alive and well at the Bernardsville Library. One hundred years later, on the anniversary of Phyllis's discovery of her dead lover, the entire event replayed itself as an audio recording. The account goes as follows: One afternoon, the lady of the house was in her front parlor doing her needlepoint as her toddler played at her feet with his toys and blocks. She heard heavy footsteps coming up the front porch, and she rose from the sofa to answer the door. Suddenly, she heard the door open. Frightened that her home was being broken into, she grabbed her son and hid behind the sofa. She heard the marching steps proceed through her house and end in the kitchen with a loud thud. Then she heard the marching steps come back toward her and exit through the front door, slamming it shut. She heard the steps fade down the front porch. Next, she heard someone running down the main staircase. She heard this person go into the kitchen. She then heard chopping sounds and a blood-curdling female scream. She grabbed her son and quickly left her home. They stayed with a neighbor until her husband, a banker in Morristown, returned home from his business trip.

When her husband found her at the neighbor's home and heard the story, he went to their home with a Morristown police officer. The officer found no signs of forced entry or exit. They concluded it was safe for the family to return home.

It's said that the sounds of the event have replayed several times on this sad anniversary. I cannot personally attest to this. I can say that while researching the Bernardsville Library as an investigation venue for the NJ Ghost Conference in 2004, I heard some interesting stories. One is that in the 1970s, the library used to close for the dinner hour. One night a part-time teenaged employee returned from her dinner break to resume work. She remained in her warm car waiting for the librarian to return and unlock the library. She happened to look up and saw a young girl sitting on top of the table in the children's section. Panicked that they had locked someone in the library, she got out of her car and ran to the front door. Sure enough, the door was locked, but fortunately the librarian was coming up the steps. The young employee said, "Hurry! We've locked a girl in there!" The librarian smiled at her coworker, calmly unlocked the door, and said, "Oh, no, dear. That's just Phyllis."

The renovations to the building in 1974 seemed to relegate the activity and sightings of Phyllis to the original portions of the structure. Her sad weeping is heard on occasion in these older parts of the library, and in 1989 a child claimed to see the ghost of a woman in a long white dress in the reading room.

In 2000, a new library was built at One Anderson Hill Road. The original structure that served as the library for ninety-five years remains at Two Morristown Road. This is the building the NJGHS investigated in 2004 and is now Sandra John Interiors. Investigating it was challenging given the number of people who wanted to participate and how cramped the space was with all the furniture, displays, fabrics, and knickknacks. We managed though. Sandra addressed our group and explained how she's experienced the movement of certain objects and her paperwork. She said she would leave a decorative item in a certain position and return hours later to find it shifted from that position, and no one who worked for her had touched it. The key spot for this shifting of items happened in the former kitchen, where Byram's coffin had been dropped onto the counter.

I split the group in two so one could head upstairs and the other could handle the first floor. Halfway through our investigation time, we switched the groups' positions. Some investigators who were tracking a weird light anomaly on their digital cameras called me back to the display room. It looked like a blue streak of light coming down from the ceiling next to the bedpost of the four-poster bed. Then the light would show up in the center of the two bedposts at the head of the bed. I took some pictures with my digital camera but did not capture any anomaly.

I went upstairs to check on that team. They were doing well navigating in the dark and with the limited space to move, but as for paranormal activity, nothing was captured. I went to the front room on the second floor. Two other investigators came in and said they were not detecting any shifts or drops in ambient temperature, and nothing abnormal was registering on the EMF meter. I took some pictures in spite of their news. The lack of anomalies in my pictures confirmed their findings.

I went back downstairs near the fireplace to look out the window and see what the view was like for the ghost who was witnessed by John Maddaluna, former Bernardsville police chief. Maddaluna was a rookie cop in the 1950s working the midnight shift. He saw a young woman in a white dress in this window. At first he thought she was a mannequin because of the way her head was turned and it appeared she was staring down. Yet he swore he saw her turn her head. He went back later that night and did not see the "mannequin." Eventually, he admitted what he saw to his sergeant, who comforted Maddaluna with, "Aw, hell, don't worry about it. I've seen her a number of times."

The time was up, and I gathered the investigators in the main hall. We thanked Sandra and made our exit. Once outside, several of us stood around chatting about the investigation and how it was on the dull side. I noted how this happens. You hear how haunted a place is, and when you get there, it's as if the ghost goes into hiding. No sooner did I make that remark than I took a picture of the building and a huge orb appeared. I immediately took another picture, but the orb was gone. I confirmed

Sandra John Interiors - 5/15/04
a ghost? Who knows...a few raindrops were just starting
as we arrived at this famous location
The original structure of the haunted Bernardsville Library

Large orb captured at the Bernardsville Library

this with those around me that I was the only one who took a picture at that moment to make sure I hadn't captured someone else's infrared beam on their autofocus camera. Maybe Phyllis was hanging around outside the whole time? After all, it was pretty crowded in there with all of us.

In 2001 I met with reporter Paul Franklin for lunch so he could interview me for his Halloween story in the *Home News Tribune*. He mentioned his all-night visit to the Bernardsville Library for a Halloween story that he wrote in 1992. Paul had reviewed the various stories about the library prior to his stay. He had asked the elderly librarian about spending the night in the library, and she had said that no one had ever stayed there alone. He thought it best at that point to invite two of his buddies along for company.

He was on time for his 1992 stay, arriving at 7:00 p.m. He waited for his friends to show up, but by 7:30 he realized they were not going to come. He set up camp in the room by the front door. He brought his sleeping bag, pillow, some food, and a CD player. His plan was to play some classical music to evoke the spirit of Phyllis while keeping his calm.

After settling in, he heard the sound of someone walking on the wooden platform outside. He figured it was his friends showing up late to scare him. He went to find them, but no one was out there. He returned to his sleeping bag and decided to converse with the spirit of Phyllis. He talked about how tragic it was to find her lover dead the way she did. He went on to coach her about how she should move on. He said this conversation was healing for him too as he had just ended a relationship. Paul said the atmosphere was calm and welcoming. He was not scared at all.

Close to 5:00 a.m., he heard a very loud bang in the room above him. He couldn't tell if it was a dresser drawer or a safe being dropped. He said it was so loud that he thought for a moment it might have been a truck going over a bump in the road with its trailer slamming down. As he was running through the various explanations for the cause of the sound in his mind, he noticed the atmosphere had begun to change. He felt threatened and paranoid. He said the energy changed to a negative presence that wanted nothing more than for him to leave. He packed up his stuff and made it to the front door. He took a quick peek to his left and to his right to see if Phyllis was standing there. Nope. He bolted out the door and made it to his car. He said he felt so relieved once he was pulling out of the parking lot. He also felt a sense of accomplishment. He had made it the whole night, alone, in a haunted library. He went home and slept.

Later that day, he went back to the library to copy some articles and question the librarian about what could have made that loud banging sound he heard. She said the room above where he was staying was completely empty. Paul told me that in his thirty-eight years as a sports reporter, the night in the Bernardsville Library was the most memorable experience of his career.

Whether history recognizes the existence of Phyllis Parker or not, the librarians still recognize her presence in the new building with the computer problems, lost data, and other electrical disturbances. They keep a library card on file for Phyllis too. I wonder whether she has ever checked out any books, or simply checked out.

Central New Jersey

MORRIS

**CENTRAL
NEW JERSEY**

HUNTERDON

UNION

RICHMOND

RARITAN
BAY

SOMERSET

MIDDLESEX

MERCER

MONMOUTH

OCEAN

Lebanon
The Fox & the Hound Tavern

Port Monmouth
Spy House

Scotch Plains
The Ghosts of Scotch Plains

Pattenburg
Pattenburg House

Raritan
Raritan Library

Summit
Blood Lane & the Suicide Water
Tower

Belvidere
Welcome to the Hotel Belvidere

Asbury Park
Harry's Roadhouse

Sayreville
Bus Crash Ghosts

Springfield
Ghosts of Baltus Roll

Perth Amboy
The Proprietary House

South Plainfield
Liquid Assets

Cranbury
Cranbury Inn

CHAPTER 20

The Fox and Hound Tavern at the Lebanon Hotel
LEBANON

THE FOX AND HOUND TAVERN is located in the Lebanon Hotel in Lebanon, at the intersection of Main Street and Cokesbury Road. Most people in New Jersey would remember it as the Cokesbury Inn. The Lebanon Hotel dates to 1820, when it was built to accommodate travelers on the newly rerouted turnpike from East Brunswick, New Jersey to Easton, Pennsylvania.

In 1923 a gas explosion killed eleven people in what was the original post office and general store across the street from the Lebanon Hotel. This prompted the formation of the Lebanon Fire Company.

A new general store and post office were built to replace the ones that were destroyed by the explosion. However, they burned down in 1980, and today it's a gravel parking lot.

Periodically it's reported that one hears frantic footsteps bounding down the staircase in the Lebanon Hotel, but no one can be observed making such sounds. They could be the residual haunting of the boarder who ran downstairs and out the door at the time of the gas explosion to offer his help.

The day I showed up to have lunch and conduct research for this chapter, I was told the restaurant was closed due to a gas leak. I'm serious as a heart attack here. The man who warned me was one of the owners, George. After I took some pictures of the outside of the building and explained to him why I was there, he said I could come inside for a cold lunch only. Food is food as far as I'm concerned. My main goal was to get face time with this owner and pump him for some paranormal dirt on the place.

George was new to the Hunterdon County area, having been here for only seven years. Originally from Jersey City, he struck me as someone with business and street smarts who had been lulled into a relaxed state by Lebanon's bucolic temperament. George and his business partner, Tom, bought the inn in 2004 and soon began massive renovations.

At first he had nothing to say about the place in a paranormal context. He told me how he had been in the building at all times of day and night during the renovations and never felt or heard anything disturbing. I'd love to say my eyes brimmed with tears of disappointment and melted his pragmatic heart to share what he experienced, but the truth is that he remembered a couple incidences on his own. George said that one night after closing, he and the bartender, Billy, were cleaning up the bar. They heard a knock on the front door. When George went to answer it, no one was there.

Another night after closing, George stayed over in one of the rooms upstairs. He said he heard some noises coming from the restaurant area below him. It sounded like people talking, although he couldn't make out their words. He didn't have a good feeling about it and decided to stay locked in his room till daybreak. When he came downstairs in the morning, everything was in place as it should have been. There were no signs of anyone having been there the night before.

I asked George about the gas leak. He said when he opened up the building in the morning, the smell of gas hit him in the face. He called the gas company and they cut the gas to the building immediately and said they would send a repair person out to investigate it. George said they did find a cracked gas pipe. He was waiting on the repairman to return and replace the broken pipe. What's truly unsettling is George said this is the second time this has happened since he's owned the place. I asked him whether he noticed anything out of the norm last night when he was closing up. He said no. The reason I asked was to figure out whether there were any ghosts at the Lebanon Hotel with a consciousness allowing them to interact with the living—and hopefully warn the owner of the gas leak or other possible danger relating to the restaurant. I was curious to see whether there was some thread of consistency between the ghostly warning systems of the Cranbury Inn and the Spy House (see Chapter 21). Perhaps an otherworldly alarm bell was rung but George didn't notice it.

Lunch arrived. I had the grilled veggie wrap. I have to say if the chef can make a cold lunch taste this good under such extreme circumstances, I can only imagine the epicurean delights he's capable of with a functioning stove. Whether you are interested in ghosts or not, dinner at the Fox and Hound Tavern should be on your list of things to do before you die.

When I was done eating, the bartender on duty was kind

enough to take me to the basement so I could take some pictures in the area below the oldest part of this building, which
George said dates to 1757, when it was a stagecoach stop, not the
formal hotel constructed in 1820. It is here where the architect
took a picture of an apparition. George told me that his architect
was taking pictures throughout the building for documentation
during the renovation. In the basement he took a photo of what
appeared to be a soldier in profile, slumped forward and holding
his rifle up against his shoulder. For some reason, I pictured
in my mind the cap on the head of this apparition as that of a
Union soldier during the Civil War. I didn't articulate this, but
the next words out of George's mouth were, "He looked like a
Civil War soldier." George said he took pictures in the same spot
with his own camera after the architect's photo shoot. He got
the same apparition in the same location. I wish I could have
seen these photos, but George was in a hurry to get to his meeting. I didn't want to impose on his time any further.

I did notice a sweet floral smell when I first went down the
basement stairs. I grew excited, thinking that maybe the ghost
of Lydia Huffman was nearby. It's reported that Lydia was the
first housekeeper at the hotel and that she made her own lavender soaps. Every so often, people catch a whiff of lavender and
take that to mean she is near. George said he's never smelled it
but that his patrons have reported it to him on occasion. By the
time I got to the basement floor, I realized a washer and dryer
were operating. Apparently the staff washes the table linens on
site. I was smelling laundry detergent.

I was not having any luck taking photos with my Nikon
Coolpix digital camera in the basement. It's said that the inn
was a stop on the Underground Railroad. When it was the
Cokesbury Inn, some employees quit after experiencing a chill
when going down the basement stairs. I admit that navigating
the stairs and uneven basement floor in three-inch slingbacks

was an adventure, but I didn't experience anything paranormal or remotely scary. I didn't even capture a dust orb.

Back on the main level, I took some pictures in hopes of capturing an orb similar to the one that I saw in a picture of the bar on the restaurant's Web site. I did capture a very small orb by the reception stand in the entrance at the foot of the staircase. I didn't bother to record for EVPs since there was too much background noise between televisions in the bar and people talking.

I also didn't get to wander upstairs, where the former boarding rooms, now offices, are located, but I would love to conduct a formal all-night investigation at the Fox and Hound. At the very least, I'm going back for dinner when I can get a hot meal.

CHAPTER 21

The Spy House
PORT MONMOUTH

THE SEABROOK-WILSON HOUSE, affectionately
known as the "Spy House" for its use in trading captured British spies for the return of American Revolutionaries, is without
a doubt the claim to haunted fame for New Jersey. It's located
on the Raritan Bay in Port Monmouth. This three-hundred-
plus-year-old structure has been touted as the number one most
haunted site on the Eastern Seaboard and in the top five haunted
locations in the United States.

Back in 1992, I had been married close to ten years to Jeff
and had our first son, Brian. In October, Halloween events began
getting publicity in the local newspapers. I liked Halloween,

especially being a mom and getting to plan and create a costume for my son. Beyond the costume and trick-or-treating, it was just another day. One morning that October, my husband came out of the reading room (most people refer to it as the bathroom) with newspaper in hand and pants at his ankles, pointing to an article in the paper and saying how we should check this out. Remember, I said we had been married close to ten years at this point. This is how married folks ask their spouse out on a date.

What Jeff was so enthusiastically pointing to was the story about ghost tours at the Spy House Museum. I scanned through and saw the dates and times and said that if we could get a sitter for that Saturday night, we could go. He returned to his reading room agreeing with me and muttering something about getting his mother to watch Brian.

Saturday night came, and there was "mama" to baby-sit Brian while Jeff and I were on our way to Exit 117 on the Garden State Parkway to find this ghost tour. Now, mind you, I had never been on a ghost tour. I was a haunted house fan and classic horror movie fan, but I knew nothing of ghost tours. That's not to say I knew nothing about ghosts. I had written my senior term paper on "ESP and Its Psychic Relations" back in high school and included a chapter on ghosts. Yet, I couldn't figure out how one gets a tour of ghosts.

So aside from the heart-in-my-throat trip swiftly down the parkway courtesy of Jeff, it was an uneventful ride. (I swear that man was a New York cabby in his past life.)

We arrived at the Spy House, went inside, and were greeted by some women sitting behind a table selling the ghost tour tickets. One tour was already in progress, we were told, and the next one would start in about thirty minutes. We bought the tickets and went into the other room, where a collection of stuffed wildlife was on display.

While perusing this room, we arrived at the fireplace. On the mantel were some pictures and odds and ends: antique tools and such. We were both studying the artifacts and pictures on the mantel when I smelled the odor of pipe tobacco. I looked at Jeff, and he was looking at me. He was thinking, "Oh, no, she's going to get a migraine, and we'll have to leave." And, I was thinking, "Oh, no, I'm going to get a migraine, and we'll have to leave and miss the tour."

Before either Jeff or I could say what we were thinking and panicking over, the smell was gone. Our expressions shifted from "Oh, crap!" to "Oh, phew!" in a matter of seconds. With that, I said, "Did you smell that?" and he replied, "Yes, I thought you were going to get a migraine." (I am sensitive to certain smells that can trigger a migraine headache.) We both thought it was weird how a smell that distinct and pungent could be there one minute and completely gone the next.

The night was young, and phase one of the ghost tour was beginning. We sat down to watch a video that starred the tour guide, Jane Doherty, as she appeared on the now defunct show *Sightings* while at the Spy House. In the video we saw how Jane channeled the ghost of "Robert the Pirate," and he disclosed burying his treasure in tunnels below the Spy House.

Jane Doherty was not just a tour guide. She was the president of the Jersey Society for Parapsychology and a professional psychic medium whose trademark talent was her stomach distending to appear ten months pregnant when in the presence of spirit energy, or a ghost. Before she began the tour, she made it a point to jiggle her stomach so we could compare its appearance then to when we got upstairs, where she always experiences Robert.

Jane said the room we were gathered in used to be the main room when Spy House was a tavern and Thomas Whitlock was the tavern owner and operator. She pointed out the taxidermy animals on the table in front of the window and told how when the museum's curator, Gertrude Niedlinger, would find these stuffed animals on the floor in a line, it meant trouble. To clarify,

Jane said that Gertrude opened up the museum one morning and found the animals in this formation. She thought it was very odd, yet as she made her way through the museum to the kitchen, she noticed a strong gas smell. The stove in the kitchen was leaking gas. She called the gas company and they dispatched a repairman immediately. He told Gertrude how the place would have blown sky high had she not discovered this leak and called.

We continued the tour through the next room and then ascended to the second floor. Jane pointed out that she would be standing in this particular corner as you came off the stairs so she could show people her distended stomach while in the spirit energy of Robert the Pirate.

While inching our way up the stairs, with Jeff on the step above mine, I got a sudden and sickening sensation of being punched in the stomach and feeling completely nauseated. I looked up at Jeff and told him I was about to toss my cookies and to please get me out of there. We both looked down the staircase only to see wall-to-wall people and no sign of an exit route.

"Laura," he said, "there's no way to get down from here." With that, he instinctively pulled me up on his step holding on to me by my elbows. My tippy toes were clinging for dear life to the edge of that step, and yet the nausea was leaving me. I felt so relieved. Then, the crowd began to move and we climbed up to the landing of the second floor.

When we made it to where Jane was illustrating her stomach distention, we had to ask her about what had just happened with my nausea. She noted that clairvoyants see a British Redcoat making his patrol at times in the very area where I had been standing. She explained that with the additions and modifications to the house over the years, the ghost patrolled according to how he remembered the building, not the way it is now. Therefore, while completing his patrol, he "walked" right through me. The clash of our energies or vibratory frequencies is what caused me to experience the "punch" and feel sick to my stomach.

I guess the best way to explain this whole vibratory frequency difference is to picture an oscillating fan. When it is shut off, you can see three solid blades. That represents us, the living. When the fan is turned on its highest speed, the fan blades appear to be invisible and you can see right through them. That is what the ghosts are like. They vibrate at such a high-rate frequency, you see right through them. It's theorized that the ghost has to learn to slow down its vibrations in order to manifest in a more solid form that we can see. Sometimes they get it so right that they appear as solid as you or I. Other times, they appear as a shadow out of the corner of your eye, or a humanoid shape of dust or a partial torso floating about.

We continued our tour of the second floor and learned about the haunted dresser in the front bedroom. Jane warned the group not to stand too close to the dresser because its negative energy causes nausea. Given what I had just been through, I made it a point to stand very far from the dresser. Also in this bedroom was a closet that had a secret stairway that led to the front room downstairs. When the place was a tavern, that was the bar area. Jane figured this was how gentleman patrons gained access to the ladies of the evening discreetly.

Across from this room was the back bedroom, where people would see the ghost of "Abigail" staring out from the one corner window toward the Raritan Bay. This was also the children's room. One tour participant who dismissed the ghost and paranormal activity in general experienced the Spy House children one night when he left the tour early. He was making his way to his truck in the lot outside when he heard the sounds of children playing. He followed the sounds to the back of the Spy House. There he saw three small children dressed in lightweight clothing running about and playing. As he approached them, he couldn't help but wonder what kind of parents would allow their children to play outside at 11 o'clock at night. As he got closer to them, they suddenly appeared in a circle around him. They were holding hands and singing "Ring Around the Rosie." At this point, the young man realized the clothing the children were dressed in was not of our time period. It appeared to be more turn-of-the-twentieth-century clothing. Now he realized that these were not children being neglected by their parents and playing outside way past their bedtime. They were ghosts. As his shock set in, the children sang, "Ashes, ashes, we all fall down" and disappeared.

This former disbeliever found his way to his truck with great haste and tore out of the parking lot. The next day he called Jane to tell her of his experience. She explained to him about the three Spy House children and how the one, a boy, likes to play with our modern-day gadgets, like wristwatches. Several ghost tour participants would notice that their watches were set incorrectly after completing the tour.

After the tour, we collected some literature on upcoming séances that Jane conducted right there at the Spy House. Jeff and I left for a diner, and our conversation over food and coffee was all about ghosts. We were both surprised to learn that the other was fascinated with this subject. In almost ten years of marriage, it had never come up. I just figured he liked old horror movies and The Twilight Zone for their scare and shock value. I never mentioned how I lived in a haunted house and did my high school senior term paper on ESP and ghosts.

We decided to attend one of Jane's séances at the Spy House the following month. It was a night right out of a Hammer horror movie. The wind was howling through the cracks and crevices of the three-hundred-year-old house. Lightning streaks lit up the sky in terrifying patterns, and thunder boomed at deafening levels. The atmospheric weather conditions would allow ghosts to draw off this energy and achieve manifestation more readily.

The chairs were arranged in a circle in the room with the taxidermy animals. As we all sat down, Jane explained how the circle would be kept together by our joining hands. She said if someone in the circle began to experience anything, she would connect the hands of the people on either side of her behind her back. This would allow her to move about the circle without breaking the energy. She noted that whenever someone in the circle experiences a change in energy or a physical ailment, it is usually a message or indicator meant for the person sitting opposite them in the circle.

Everyone was quiet as Jane asked for protective white light and invited the spirit world to join our circle. Within a few minutes, a young woman became very dizzy and leaned forward. Jane made her way to the woman and asked her what she was experiencing. Through her gasps for air, she said that she felt like she was falling down a roller coaster at great speed and it was making her very dizzy and nauseated.

Jane turned to look at the people across the circle from this woman and asked if anyone had a loved one who died in a plane accident. Sure enough, one woman said her father died in a plane crash. He was the pilot of a little Cessna.

Jane was able to guide the woman through the entire experience of the plane crash to relay the information to the woman across the circle who lost her father in this accident. Once the message was completed, the woman who experienced the crash had to be carried out to the front porch for some air and to recuperate from the sickening experience. Jane closed the circle for this break.

Before we began the next circle, Jane had to flip over the cassette tape in her recorder. She commented aloud that she hoped to transcribe the tapes from all the Spy House séances some day.

We began the séance again with Jane calling out for white light protection and inviting any spirits to participate in our circle. After a few minutes, I began to feel a pressure on the left side of my neck that was forcing my head to lean to the right. I dismissed this as a crick in my neck from sitting so still. However, the pressure began to build to the point where I could no longer ignore it. I spoke up and let Jane know what I was feeling. By the time she was standing in front of me, my head was so bent over that my right ear was almost pinned to my right shoulder. Jane could sense an energy or spirit around me. She called out to the people sitting opposite me in the circle. She asked if any of them had lost a loved one to a stroke. One woman spoke up saying her father was found dead on the kitchen floor with his head bent over to the right from a severe stroke. This confirmed that this spirit energy was indeed her father coming through. Jane was able to channel the answers to the woman's questions of her father. The father's spirit revealed that the money his daughters were looking for was hidden in a coffee can on a shelf in the garage. The woman and her sisters yelled "Maxwell House!" in unison, and with that the spirit energy released me. I was able to move my head back to center. What a relief!

After the séance, I approached Jane and offered to transcribe the tapes for her in exchange for Jeff and I being able to attend future séances at the Spy House. She said to call her office on Monday and follow up.

After some phone tag with Jane's office voicemail, I finally got the job of transcribing the cassette tapes in exchange for attending séances and going on ghost hunts with her. One day while transcribing a tape of a Spy House séance, I heard the voice of a little girl say, "I don't like that man. Mommy, he's scaring me." I stopped the tape, rewound it and played it again. I still heard this voice. I thought to myself, "Who would bring their kid to a séance?"

As I continued the transcription, I heard the little girl's voice say, "He's making me laugh," and she giggled as well. At the conclusion of the séance, I heard the little girl say, "Can we go now?"

When Jeff and his mother returned from running errands, I played the parts of the tape for them on the stereo in the living room. Jeff was shocked, like I was, by the thought that someone would bring their kid to a séance. As he listened to all the parts where this little one's voice was heard, he looked at me and said, "No one ever answers her." I explained to him that perhaps the parent was just nodding her head in response. Yet that wouldn't explain why, during the height of the séance, no one else in the room even snickered or commented when the little girl spoke.

It was interesting to note that the point where the little girl said, "He's scaring me" was the part where Jane sensed a male energy wearing a black cape and top hat that came in from the corner of the room.

Finally, I called Jane and asked her who brought their child to one of her séances. She quickly responded with, "No one! No one under eighteen is allowed to participate in the séances." I told her about the voice of a little girl on the tape. She was intrigued, to say the least.

When I finished transcribing, I returned the tape and printout to Jane. To this day, I kick myself for not making a copy of that tape because that was the best EVP I've ever heard. I was such a novice ghost hunter, I didn't realize that I had a Class A EVP in my hands.

Years later, I was still successful with finding ghosts at the Spy House. I went there with a television crew while filming our investigation on the surrounding grounds. I recorded an unusual temperature reading on the thermal scanner in that the temperature of the upstairs window was colder than the temperature of the window on the first floor below it. Since heat rises, this should not have been the case. Perhaps it was Abigail standing in that upstairs window that was causing the temperature to be twenty degrees colder? I'll never know for sure as no photograph or video taken revealed any anomalies of that sort.

However, this same night, Laura Lindemann, team leader for the Northeast Division of the NJGHS, acquired an EVP saying "Oh, no!" over by the well on the property of the Spy House.

I have been inside the Spy House only once since it was turned into offices for the Parks Department. That was a Saturday afternoon when my kids and I took a ride down to see the place. We walked around the house and found a little baby bird displaced from its nest. Fortunately, a Parks & Recreation officer was there, and she opened up the Spy House to look inside for a ladder so she could return the little bird to safety. Of course I couldn't resist stepping into the place while she hunted about for a ladder. The place was vacant for the most part. In my mind's eye, I could still see the taxidermy animals in front of the window in the main room, I could see the ghost tour check-in table, and I briefly relived the experience of smelling the pipe in front of the fireplace.

The officer could not find a ladder, and we had to pretend that she would "take care of the bird" for the sake of sparing my young son's heart from breaking at the baby bird's inevitable fate.

It's been rumored that the Spy House will reopen as a museum once more. I think that is mostly wishful thinking on the part of the many ghost hunters vying to get in there. Yet it is still worth the trip, especially on a fully moonlit night. Perhaps you'll see the three ghost children at play? Maybe you'll witness Abigail staring out the upstairs window? You might even capture some EVP of the ghosts partying in the front room from days long passed when Thomas Whitlock was the tavern owner. If nothing else, you'll have bragging rights for having braved the most haunted site on the Eastern Seaboard on the night of the full moon.

CHAPTER 22

The Ghosts of Scotch Plains
SCOTCH PLAINS

SEVERAL GHOST SITINGS IN SCOTCH PLAINS
make it a noteworthy stop on your ghosthunting tour. Next to the
Baptist Church cemetery, which is believed to be haunted, is a
New Jersey Transit bus stop that reportedly shelters a ghostly bus
rider (above photo). There are also reports of the ghost of a boy
who was hit by a stage coach as well as ghosts from suicides.

Scotch Plains dates to 1684 with the Scottish immigrants
who settled here under the leadership of George Scot. The
original name was Scot's Plains. As the town grew, main roads
were added. Park Avenue was the main thoroughfare running

through the middle of town. In 1720 William Darby donated property to build a meetinghouse and cemetery, and the Baptist Church was dedicated in 1747. John Surton built his tavern in 1737, and by 1769 it was a stagecoach stop on the Swift Sure Stage line. It became known as the Stage House Inn.

In the early days of the NJGHS, we held our monthly meetings at the Community Room in Westfield. During a meeting's "Share and Scare" segment, an attendee asked whether I knew anything about the ghost boy on Park Avenue. I wasn't familiar with the story, so this gentleman came to the front of the room to speak about it. He said that back when Scotch Plains still had unpaved roads and the stagecoach made its stops by the Stage House Inn, there was a tragic accident. A boy, whose age he did not even guess at, ran across Park Avenue as the stagecoach was approaching. The coach could not stop in time, and it hit and killed him. He also said that it happened just before the stagecoach would have reached the Stage House Inn (as one would travel today on Park Avenue from Snuffy's Restaurant toward Fanwood). He concluded that on the anniversary of this incident, motorists lock up their breaks for fear of hitting this boy they see running out onto Park Avenue, and some even end up driving right through the apparition.

Other people at the meeting chimed in to say they had heard this story too but had never witnessed it actually happen. I have driven down Park Avenue at different hours of the day or night and never witnessed this myself, but I was curious to find out more. Particularly, I would like to know this supposed anniversary date.

Around this same area in Scotch Plains is the Baptist Church and cemetery. Some NJGHS members from the town told me that there was a tradition for Halloween. There is a grave of a woman who, for whatever reason, did not like children. When trick-or-treating, the local children would leave some of their candy on her gravestone to prevent her ghost from attacking them and taking all their candy.

A small group of NJGHS members gathered to investigate this Baptist church cemetery back in 1999. The cemetery is surrounded by the town's hustle and bustle being bordered by Park and Mountain avenues. Yet once we were inside the cemetery, it was unnervingly still and quiet. Lisa and her son Scott went to the far corner of the cemetery and placed their analog cassette recorder on one of the gravestones. I went in the opposite direction to leave my cassette recorder on a gravestone as well. The members and I stayed within eyesight of each other, but far enough apart to avoid disrupting each other's recordings. I remember being over by a tree and having the most unsettling feeling. I was scared to the point of heading closer to another investigator so I wouldn't be alone.

When it came time to leave, I made sure I had everyone, but I was halfway home when I realized I had left the audio recorder in the cemetery. I had to turn around to go back and get it. This was unbelievably frightening to me. I parked the car in the church lot under a beaming pink light. I didn't shut the car off. I got out and went as fast as I could to the corner where I left the recorder. I found it and ran back to the car and got out of there. To this day, I don't know why and can't explain how such a small cemetery in the middle of town can be so intimidating.

The next day Lisa called me to say she had an EVP from the cemetery. She said it was of a person whistling. Neither of us remembered hearing anyone whistling while we were investigating. In fact, she even commented at the conclusion of the hunt how eerily quiet the cemetery seemed to be. She played the recording over the phone for me to hear. It was very clear and yet totally unrecognizable. It wasn't the typical whistling sound one makes out in public to gain someone's attention. It wasn't a recognizable tune. It was just this nondescript, vague whistle.

I went through my recording and did not have the whistling sound or any other EVPs. It was a clear recording of cars passing by on the street and people walking on the sidewalk just outside the cemetery gate. Later in the afternoon I picked up my photos from Walgreens. There were a couple of orb pictures, but they were very faint because the flash did not reach far enough. Lisa and Scott went back to this cemetery a couple of times but never captured the whistling sound again.

On the other side of the fence for this cemetery on Mountain Avenue is the New Jersey Transit bus stop complete with waiting booth and bench seating. When I used to do the Morbid Mobile Tours, in the hearse, this site was part of the tour as we had to drive right past it to head up to "Thirteen Bumps Road." The story goes that a young woman is waiting for the bus. When it pulls up, she gets on the bus and walks half way down the bus's center aisle and vanishes. I never saw any ghostly girl waiting at this stop in all the times I've driven by it, hearse or no hearse, but so many people told me about it at the NJGHS meetings that I had to include it in the tour and in this book.

Speaking of "Thirteen Bumps Road," as you drive this road, it ascends the crest of the Watchung Mountains. Over the years, it has been paved and repaved only to have these thirteen bumps resurface. It's said that a coven of witches lived on this part of the mountain. They kept to themselves. Back in the early farming days of Scotch Plains, there was a poor harvest. The failure of the crops was blamed on the witches. Supposedly the townsfolk hanged all thirteen witches and buried them in shallow graves on what is now Johnston Road. Tradition says that when you drive this road, you have to count all thirteen bumps. Any missing bumps translate to the number of witches' ghosts that have risen from their graves to terrorize you.

While doing Morbid Mobile Tours, we would give the tourists two chances to count the bumps. We would drive up the road, make a U-turn and drive back down the road. Usually, on the way back down the road, as people were busy trying to count the bumps, my then husband would shut the headlights off and slam on the breaks. It's amazing that something so simple worked every time. People freaked out at first and then laughed.

Truth to tell, the bumps were not all that discernable. There are bumps, but not significant ones of thirteen consecutively. One explanation I read about the bumps seems most logical. The bumps were intentionally installed in the road to prevent horse-drawn carriages from slipping down the steep grade of the road.

I was still curious, however, about the history of the ghost boy on Park Avenue. I could not find any information or record about a child's death by the impact of a stagecoach or wagon. I did discover a report about the death of a woman on the train tracks that could account for the ghost girl at the bus stop. At 5:00 a.m. on December 19, 1902, the crew of the New York paper train found the body of Susan Gassner on the New Jersey Central Railroad tracks by the Park Avenue Bridge. The article said she was suffering from "nervous prostration." She had left the day before to do some Christmas shopping, and when she didn't come home, her husband phoned the police. Gassner and the bus stop ghost have transportation in common. The minor discrepancy in this, for me, is that Gassner was thirty-four years old at the time of her suicide. Given the descriptions of the bus stop ghost being a "girl" or young woman, I'm not quite sure this fits. In 1902, cosmetics and hair coloring weren't what they are today. A thirty-four-year-old back then could look like a fifty-four-year-old by today's standards.

A woman named Louise Kramer would have fit the description being twenty years old at the time she made the newspaper, but she did not die when Frank Huber shot her on May 28, 1902. Her jaw was broken, and there was a hole in her cheek where the bullet exited. She was treated in Muhlenberg Hospital in Plainfield. Huber, forty years old, asked Louise to marry him repeatedly. He was a widower and father of three children from Altoona, Pennsylvania. Huber had been rejected for the last time. He bought a pistol in Newark and returned to Scotch Plains to kill Louise. He was, at least, successful in killing himself after he thought he had killed Louise.

I came across another suicide for Scotch Plains: William Murray. It's not mentioned in the article how old Murray was when he shot himself. It does say that he worked in New York City. He was a bank teller for the Empire Trust Bank. He arrived at work around 9:00 a.m. on December 5, 1908. Within an hour he was back on the train to Westfield because he felt ill. When he arrived in Westfield, he took a cab. As the cab was entering Scotch Plains, the cabby heard a gunshot. He pulled over, jumped out, and opened the back door. Murray was dead.

In 1930, there was a bus crash in Scotch Plains, but it was Salvadore Pelle of Plainfield who died while nine others were injured.

I hit one historical dead end after another. Suicides, attempted murder, a bus crash, but not one of these would match up with the ghosts reported in Scotch Plains. I know there were several people from the town who spoke of these hauntings at various NJGHS meetings. I also know that the cemetery we investigated generated some substantial orb pictures and the EVP of the whistling.

I think it's worth keeping an eye on the bus stop each time you drive by. It can't hurt to drive carefully down Park Avenue in case the ghost boy makes his run in front of your car. Have your camera ready.

CHAPTER 23

Pattenburg House

PATTENBURG

THE TOWN OF PATTENBURG in Hunterdon County has its share of history and ghosts. The name of the town reflects the U.S. patent granted to the local apple-jack distilleries. There were eight distilleries in this township during the 1870s. The advantageous location of the Lehigh Valley Railroad made for easy distribution of the liquor to Trenton and Philadelphia.

Pattenburg House was established in 1872, concurrent with the installation of the Lehigh Valley Railroad stop in town. The first floor served as a restaurant and tavern. The second floor was an inn with overnight accommodations, and the third floor was for storage.

Initially the railroad was for freight only. It wasn't until 1875 that a passenger station was built at Pattenburg. The construction of a passenger line was made possible by the building of a tunnel through Jugtown Mountain, which today is known as West Portal. Called Musconetcong Tunnel, it was the scene of the infamous Pattenburg Riot on September 22, 1872. Thomas Call was found beaten to death near the mouth of the tunnel early that morning. It ignited racial tensions between Irish and black workers. A mob of Irish workers gathered together and torched the shanty of the black workmen by the tunnel. This forced the occupants to run to the neighboring shanty, known as Black Springs, which was about one mile east of the tunnel.

The mob pursued them and ended up killing Dennis Powel, Benjamin Dismal, and Oscar Bruce. These men were buried in unmarked graves in a company-owned field.

By 1875 the Musconetcong Tunnel and the Pattenburg train station were completed. Four trains daily carried passengers, and three of those trains contained mail. To their credit, the mail was tossed from the train as the outgoing mail, fixed to the mail hang, was plucked as the train drove by. With hand sorting of the mail on the train while in transit, the mail made it from Pattenburg to New York City on the same day.

The Lehigh Valley Railroad built an amusement park called Bellewood Park in 1902. The park was located just under a mile from the Pattenburg train station. Pattenburg House became a summer vacation destination and weekend resort. Bellewood Park was known for its grand Ferris wheel, which was dismantled along with the other rides when the park closed down in 1916. Pattenburg House fell into decline after the closing of Bellewood.

The Musconetcong Tunnel was the scene of more tragedy when two men were crushed to death while working in there in 1916. Paddy Amosd and Dominick Carallais did not escape

the work train that backed onto them. Two other men, Thomas
Ruple and George Campino, were seriously injured in the accident as well.

In 1927 a larger, wider tunnel was built by Bates & Rodgers
of Cleveland to accommodate the increased traffic of the Lehigh
Valley line. With the advancements in engineering and machin-
ery, the new tunnel was constructed more easily—though not
without injuries or fatalities. On October 29, Allen Morrison
lit the fuse setting off six charges of dynamite to blast open the
pathway for the new tunnel. The fuse was defective, and before
Morrison and eight other workers could reach safety, the deto-
nation occurred. Morrison was killed instantly by a rock that
crushed his skull. The other men had to push their way through
the cloud of debris to exit the tunnel while carrying two seriously injured men.

Morrison was from Scotland and had no family in the United
States, but his body was laid to rest stateside, in Flemington.
The mile-long tunnel was completed in 1928 and was the widest
tunnel in the world at the time.

There was a passenger train trapped in the tunnel for six
hours in May 1940. The storms that raged over northwest Hunterdon County and southeast Warren County at that time caused
the "Great Slides" of earth and rock. The first slide blocked the
tracks on the west end of the tunnel. The train still had its last
car protruding from the tunnel and was going to back out when
the second slide at the east end blocked the tracks. Finally, a
track was cleared, and the 7:19 p.m. "John Wilkes" train pulled
into Easton at 1:20 a.m.

The Lehigh Valley train line suffered a dramatic loss in rid-
ership over the years. The last passenger service was conducted
on February 3, 1961. Today the tracks are long gone from the
Musconetcong Tunnel, and a large crater surrounded by a chain
link fence is all that remains of Bellewood Park.

In 2007 I was searching for a place to record the Halloween show of our podcast, *The Deadline*. I was looking for a place like the Stanhope House that is a restaurant and bar and haunted. Someone suggested Pattenburg House. I contacted the staff, but they were not able to accommodate us. I more or less forgot about the place until I was interviewing Amy Connolly about the Stanhope House and she mentioned she used to waitress at Pattenburg House and that it is extremely haunted.

Amy told me that in the short time she worked at Pattenburg House, there was paranormal activity almost daily. She told me that there was a ghost customer that employees would see sitting at the bar. He had on a plaid shirt and was so solid that the bartenders would ask him, "What can I get you?" Of course, they'd turn around to serve him and he would be gone. I couldn't help but wonder if this was the ghost of Allen Morrison. Granted, he died in the tunnel, but what's to say his spirit didn't decide to belly up to the local bar just as he may have done in life?

When I spoke with Barbara Heinrichs, the former chef at Pattenburg House, she confirmed the sighting of the ghostly man in the plaid shirt at the bar. She admitted she never saw him herself, but she remembers several of the bartenders and wait staff discussing his visits.

Barbara did see a ghost at Pattenburg House while working there from 1986 to 1999. She was at her station in the kitchen, and she could see the back door and its vestibule area with her peripheral vision. She saw a young woman come in the door. This young woman had on a long white dress and had long dark hair. Barbara said she could see the young girl come in the back door, cross out of view as if heading over to the coat hooks in the vestibule to hang her coat, and then leaning backwards enough to pop her head half way into the doorway of the kitchen before making her way to the bar area. Barbara thought the girl was the young waitress on staff named India. But she couldn't help thinking, "Why would India come to work in a white dress?"

After ten minutes or so, Barbara went into the bar area to ask India about the white dress. When she got to the bar, only the bartender on duty was there. Barbara asked him if he saw India come in. He said, "No." Barbara told him that she saw some young girl come in the back door, hang up her coat, and head for the bar area. The bartender told her that he was the only one in the place besides her at that time. He quipped, "You must have seen the ghost."

Barbara said she was so unnerved by this that she went to the Hunterdon County Library to research the area after work. She knew what she had seen. She came across an article in the *Hunterdon County Democrat* newspaper about a young girl who committed suicide on the railroad tracks not far from Pattenburg House in the 1940s or 1950s. In all the research that was done for this book, I didn't find any such article or mention of any suicides near Pattenburg along the tracks.

As the sightings of the man at the bar increased, along with other phenomena such as inexplicable cold spots, the younger employees began to play with a Ouija board at Pattenburg House after closing. Barbara said she sat in on a couple of their sessions. She was curious to learn about this suicide girl. In one such session, Barbara asked for the spirit of the girl to come through. There is no way to validate whether this was the actual spirit of the girl who killed herself. As I said, I found no articles in the local papers or the *New York Times* regarding a suicide in the Pattenburg area of the Lehigh Valley train tracks. Barbara said the spirit replied that when she was sixteen years old, she had worked at Pattenburg House. After being raped at work, she was so distraught that she took her life by stepping in front of an oncoming train. It makes for a great story but, again, is not verifiable.

Most days Barbara was tired at the end of her shift and went home, unlike the younger crowd that remained to play with the Ouija board. She noticed that when they operated the Ouija board, the candles would flicker wildly, doors would open and close by themselves, and the planchette would move violently about the board.

Of course playing with a Ouija board is just asking for trouble. The board itself is a low-vibratory-frequency tool. It taps into the less desirable psychic realm. Every case I've investigated that has some demonic or severely negative forces at work, beyond that of a ghost or haunting, always traces back to someone in the household playing with a Ouija board. I can't stress enough not to use this "game." In fact, after you finish this book, read *Ouija: The Most Dangerous Game*, by Stoker Hunt.

Pattenburg House has changed hands in the last few years. I spoke with Robin, a part-time employee. She works in the bar and kitchen areas. Robin said that just a few months ago she felt she was touched while on the third floor. She turned to see who it was that wanted her attention, but no one was there. She said that experience is shared by many of the employees who venture up to the third floor. Robin said she thinks it's the ghost of the young woman, a general's daughter, who hanged herself on the third floor. She said that this girl was teaching a young male slave to read. When it came to light, a crowd hanged the young slave out in front of Pattenburg House. The young girl was heartbroken, and at midnight she hanged herself.

Again, in the all the research I've done, nothing appeared about this story. I spoke with Hunterdon County Park Ranger and local history buff Doug Kiovsky, and he said the only Hunterdon County general he knew of was named Taylor, and he was killed in 1863 in the Civil War.

Robin told me that this story was detailed on the Pattenburg House Web site. It wasn't. In fact, the site's URL redirects to a MySpace page (http://www.myspace.com/pattenburghouse), and no historical information is mentioned there.

It is frustrating for a paranormal investigator to hear various warped and contorted versions of ghost stories and not be able to verify them. More than likely, this tragic tale of the girl killing herself was concocted from one of the imaginations of the Ouija board participants or some pseudo-psychic who dined at Pattenburg House and claimed to have a vision.

Robin went on to say that the paranormal activity experienced at Pattenburg House seems heightened whenever the owner is on vacation. While she works there only on Sunday afternoons, she said that other employees have noticed this pattern as well. The present owner did not return my call for an interview.

Mulhockaway Creek, which runs close by Pattenburg House, could amplify paranormal activity there, as water sources typically do. There is not much left in Pattenburg from its heyday save for Pattenburg House: it's no wonder the ghosts choose to convene there. While plaid shirts are not high on my list of fashion favorites, I'll be sure to refrain from commenting if I see a man at Pattenburg House bar wearing one. I will, however, take his picture.

CHAPTER 24

The Raritan Library
RARITAN

THERE'S MORE TO CHECK OUT THAN JUST BOOKS and media at the Raritan Library of Somerset County. This building's oldest section dates to the early 1700s. It became known as "The Homestead" when General John Frelinghuysen owned it. Over the years, it went through expansions and renovations to reach its present-day Federal style of architecture. It also changed ownership over the years but ended with its purchase by Peter H. B. Frelinghuysen in 1970. He donated it to the Borough of Raritan for use as a museum and public library.

I visited the library in February 1996 shortly after the media blitz about it being haunted. I wanted to see for myself what was up with this library. In one newspaper article, it was described as being actively haunted and having books that flew off the shelves. The framed picture of John Frelinghuysen that was secured to a tabletop mysteriously fell to the floor and broke into three pieces.

Another newspaper article completely dismissed the haunting by saying it was a feeble attempt to get notoriety and ultimately more funding to cover its budget overruns and construction costs. I admit reading this article did blow a lot of holes in the haunting theory. The ghostly aroma of Old Spice aftershave attributed to General Frelinghuysen was actually the sickeningly sweet and spicy air fresheners used to cover the foul odor of backed-up toilets caused by poor plumbing.

Apparently the now defunct paranormal investigative team known as the Unexplained Phenomena Investigators spent the night in the library in 1996 and concluded the place was haunted. Anita DiNizio, the library's director at that time, published UPI's findings, and the media jumped on it. From Telemundo to news radio, reporters descended on the tiny library like bees on flowers.

I visited the library with camera in hand. While snooping upstairs, I found the little picture of Frelinghuysen that supposedly crashed to the floor. It appeared to have been returned to its frame and in sound condition. I took a picture of it. I was using a 35mm camera, so I did not have the instantaneous results of digital. This was also back in the day when it was still unwise to come right out and announce oneself as a ghost hunter.

I toured the upstairs and took note of any drafts or cold spots. I honestly don't remember feeling any. Again, this was long before I had a thermal scanner to detect these fluctuations and register them. I hoped to experience *something* paranormal, a smell or a cold spot, but I really didn't encounter anything.

I went down to the children's section, which is the oldest

part of the library. I am not sure whether it's the age of the place or what, but I definitely *felt* something there. I was drawn to the fireplace, which had been outfitted with shelving for books. I took some pictures as best I could without drawing attention to myself. I ducked in and out of the rows of books hoping to see one fly off the shelf at me. That didn't happen.

The library staff reported hearing strange noises such as footsteps when no one was around to account for them. They smelled cigarette smoke even though it was strictly prohibited in the library. They felt drafts where windows were not present. I took all this into account as I wandered through the library taking pictures and listening intently for more than the typical whispers of "your book is due back on . . ."

The next day, I received my prints from this expedition, and there was nothing but nice pictures of the inside of a library. No orbs. No apparitions. I attributed this to being there in the daytime as opposed to camping out at night alone when it's quiet. I never did get the opportunity to do that.

I did get to speak with well-known psychic Jane Doherty about her experience with the Raritan Library. She went there in 1996 at the height of the commotion and sat outside the library the first day waiting to meet a reporter. She kept staring at the cannon in the front yard. Jane noticed there was a spirit energy or mist around the cannon. She watched it intently. It would be there one minute and gone the next. After about an hour of waiting, she left. She returned home to get a message that explained the reporter had mixed up his appointments. She went back to the library the next day and waited again for the reporter. She watched the energy mist appear and disappear around the cannon. Finally, the reporter arrived, and they went inside to conduct the interview.

The reporter was intent on seeing Jane's famous stomach protract in the presence of spirit energy or a ghost. Jane said they walked throughout the library. She sensed a male energy upstairs and "saw" a uniform. She related this presence to that of General Frelinghuysen. She detected a female spirit energy while upstairs. This unidentified spirit has been seen staring out the window, reportedly, by people on the street.

Jane said the strongest area for energy that she detected was in the oldest part of the library by the fireplace. As she entered this room, she saw a book sticking out from the shelf as if it were ready to fall to the floor. She went over and drew it from the shelf. The title of this book was *How to Write a Ghost Story*. Jane said she laughed to herself, thinking, "What are the chances?"

In 2006 Jane went back with a reporter who was covering several haunted sites in Somerset County. She said she was perplexed when she arrived and didn't see the cannon out front. She was using that as her landmark to find the library. Once inside, Jane inquired about the missing cannon to one of the librarians. The librarian responded that there never was a cannon on the property. Jane figured this woman probably started working at the library after the cannon had been removed for whatever reason, so she approached another librarian and asked her. This librarian said she had worked at the library for the past fifteen years and there never was a cannon on the property.

Jane told me to this day she doesn't know what to make of the whole cannon episode. The fact that she saw it vividly two days in a row only to be told ten years later that it was never there is just confounding.

A friend of mine recently visited the Raritan Library to find out whether there were any updates on paranormal activity, knowing I was writing this book. The librarian he spoke with, Mary Anne, said the staff is, for the most part, quite at ease with the discarnate sounds of footsteps and occasional cold spots. She did mention an instance where a young boy was frightened while at the library with his mother. The mother was at the circulation

desk with her young son when he began to tremble and point at
the far corner of the room. When she asked him what the matter
was, he replied, "The old man won't stop staring at me."

There may have been financial difficulties in the library's
past, and possibly some mismanagement; but I tend to lean
more toward there being a viable haunting here. Jane Doherty
is a very credible psychic, and a child calls it like he sees it. The
Raritan Library is rich with history, architecture, and at least
two ghosts worth "checking out."

CHAPTER 25

Blood Lane and Suicide Tower

WATCHUNG RESERVATION

NEW JERSEY HAS SOME WEIRD STREET NAMES: Shades of Death Road and Gallows Hill Road are just two examples. Blood Lane, however, is not the official name of a road in the Watchung Reservation in Union County. It is a nickname given though urban legend. The road's true name is W. R. Tracy Drive, and the section in question is the bend in the road just before the bridge by Surprise Lake.

The story goes that joy-riding teenagers who were out late one night decided to cut through the Watchung Reservation. This is not a shortcut when you consider the winding road, lack of streetlights, and the 25 mph speed limit. Yet there they were, speeding into the "Res" from Glenside Avenue. They lost control of the car and crashed just before the bridge. Legend says that if you drive your car down this road at midnight on the night of a full moon, you will see the road turn blood-red in the moonlight.

Truth be told, it is an urban legend. While it made for a great scare during my Morbid Mobile Tours days in "Baby" the hearse, my research concluded that no such accident ever occurred in the Watchung Reservation. But this particular legend can be traced to an actual accident that happened nearby.

A fatal car crash involving Chatham High School teenagers took place in Florham Park on Sunday, August 12, 1984. Peter Stoesser, age seventeen, was driving his refinished 1969 Mercedes-Benz. His friends Chris Crucilla, seventeen, David Bringard, sixteen, and Thomas Horner, seventeen, were with him. All four boys were at Crucilla's house and left around 10:30 p.m. to go to Burger King in Madison. On the way, they picked up Joanne Jackowsky, seventeen. At approximately 11:22 p.m., Peter failed to negotiate the sharp turn in the road on Passaic Avenue and crashed into a four-foot-high stone wall. At the time of the accident, the pavement was wet from an earlier rainstorm. Chris Crucilla was able to climb out of the wreckage and walk the mile home to Chatham. He told his father what happened, and his father called the police. They used the Jaws of Life to free the teens from the wreckage.

Stoesser was pronounced dead at the scene. Bringard was pronounced dead on arrival at Overlook Hospital in Summit. Jackowsky was pronounced dead on arrival at St. Barnabas Medical Center in Livingston. Horner was listed in critical condition upon his arrival at St. Barnabas, and Crucilla was treated for his injuries at Morristown Memorial Hospital.

I used to work in a building very close to the scene of this accident. The stone wall actually marked the property line of the gorgeous center-hall, colonial-style house, which had been converted into offices with a warehouse built on the back. So I know this road very well. I've never formally investigated the area. Honestly, it hits a little too close to home for me since I was a senior at Chatham High School when four of these teens were freshman. I don't think I could remain objective. Should one decide to stake out this area for an investigation, I would advise extreme caution. It truly is a dangerous curve and the lighting is still sorely lacking.

After taking a drive down Blood Lane, continue up through the Watchung Reservation and take the second right after entering the circle. Not too far up on the left is a clearing to pull into and park. There is a hiking trail to follow here that takes you to the 150-foot "Suicide Tower." This is technically the Watchung Water Tower in Mountainside. When I was a kid in the 1970s, my father used to take my brother and me to this water tower. There was a staircase that wound its way up the outside of the tower. Once at the top, we had an amazing view of the New York City skyline and the towns of Mountainside, Springfield, and Westfield below.

Suicide Tower got its name in 1975 when Gregg Sanders, fifteen, jumped to his death from the top of the tower. Gregg was described as a happy teenager and a successful student at Pingry, an elite private high school then located in Hillside. He lived with his parents and older sister, Wendy, who was a stellar student, musician, and valedictorian of her high school class. Their father, Thomas, was a vice president at First National City Bank in New York, and his mother, Janice, was a teacher in the church day care center. To complete this pristine, upper-class, suburban picture, they lived at 1090 Sunny Slope Drive in Mountainside in a $70,000 house complete with a kidney-shaped pool and a cabana.

Gregg maintained good grades, mostly Bs, but he was under

Suicide Tower, 1970s (Watchung Tower)

pressure to live up to his sister's academic achievement. He enjoyed sports and was on the football team at school. But Gregg had a darker side. He had a secret room adjacent to his bedroom that he could access through a hole in the wall beneath his desk. This ten-foot-long, four-foot-high room was a crawl space above the porch. Inside he had an array of swastikas, empty liquor bottles, and a hand-written collection of quotes from Adolf Hitler. He also kept a mattress and canteens full of water in this room.

In addition to the pressure Gregg had from his parents to succeed like his sister, he was scared that a recent reprimand from his history teacher during class would result in a note being sent home. According to a *New York Times* report, he told his friend that he had three options: "I can beat up the teacher,

Suicide Tower today

I can intercept the letter, or I can kill myself."

On January 15, 1975, Gregg's English composition titled "Father Knows Best" was read aloud to the class. The teacher praised the imaginary conversation between Jesus and God taking place between the crucifixion and resurrection and recommended it for the school's literary magazine. Gregg left school that day like any other. Once he was home, he sat down and wrote his suicide note, beginning with "To Whom It May Concern." Included in this note was the explanation of why he had to kill his parents to spare them the pain of living through his suicide.

At about 9:30 in the evening, Gregg entered the dining room with an ax and attacked his father. His father made it as far as the kitchen, where he died from a final blow to the back of his skull. Gregg's mother came downstairs to the dining room to see what the commotion was and received a fatal blow from Gregg's ax. Gregg left his note on his desk with the desk lamp shining on it. He ran out of the house in fifteen-degree weather wearing only a light shirt and khaki pants.

Gregg went to the water tower and climbed to the top. Once there, he slit his left wrist and jumped to his death. Around 11:15 p.m., four teenagers who were approaching the tower discovered Gregg's body. His parents' bodies were discovered when the police arrived at their home to tell them of Gregg's death.

After the suicide, the lower portion of the staircase was removed, making it impossible to climb the tower. The Suicide Tower had its reputation solidified as a haunted spot not only because of Gregg's suicide but also because of reports of satanic cults practicing in the woods of the Watchung Reservation.

As a teenager, I heard the stories of these cults and of a huge pentagram painted on top of the tower. In 1981, some friends and I ascended to the top, courtesy of a ladder one friend had brought along to reach the portion of the stairs still on the side of the tower. I didn't see any pentagram up there. Of course, it was dark, the only lighting being that from an occasional cigarette.

The height of the tower and climbing a ladder in the dark were scary. Accomplishing this task without being noticed by law enforcement officers was definitely scary. Did I see any ghostly apparitions or residual haunting replays of Gregg's leap to death? No. Would I ever attempt to climb the tower again? Hell, no!

I went back to the tower at night to investigate it specifically for this book. I had permission from the Union County Parks Department to be there after sunset. The hike up this trail seemed much longer than I remember. I took some pictures and digital audio recordings hoping to capture something identifiable as the spirit of Gregg Sanders. I managed to capture an orb in one of the pictures, but I knew that it wouldn't reproduce well in print. Honestly, I was scared of encountering a bear. I took a few more pictures and left. When I reviewed the audio at home, no EVPs were captured.

I've driven through the Watchung Reservation late at night with the fog eerily rolling across the road. With my overactive imagination, I half expected something to appear before my car. Nothing ever did. Still, a midnight ride down Blood Lane and an afternoon stroll up to the Suicide Tower are welcomed breaks from mundane trips to the mall.

CHAPTER 26

Welcome to the Hotel Belvidere

BELVIDERE

IF YOU'RE LIKE ME, you factor into your criteria for a weekend getaway a place that is haunted. I say skip the mini-bar, and bring on the ghosts. The Hotel Belvidere is the perfect respite from the harried life of work, Little League, and other obligations. The town of Belvidere is scenic with its Victorian homes surrounding the central park. The area is full of relaxing things to do, from antique shopping, golfing, and whitewater rafting on the Delaware River, to visiting wineries and Revolutionary War battlefields. Established in 1831, the Hotel Belvidere provides the standard features of comfort and convenience: air conditioning and Internet access—and the not-so-standard feature of ghosts.

In February 2008 I received a message from Adam Deutsch concerning the Hotel Belvidere. He is the son of the owners, Sidney and Alma Deutsch, and was "holding down the fort" while his parents were away on vacation. In Adam's message he said he suspected the hotel to be haunted and wanted to know how the NJGHS investigates. When I returned his call, we agreed to meet around 2 p.m. on February 27.

It was a bright sunny day and unseasonably warm for February when I arrived. Adam greeted me and took me to his office so we could sit and chat. I recorded the conversation as well as took notes. As much as I wanted accuracy of my notes with a recording, I wanted to capture an EVP even more. Adam began by telling me how he found this building for sale and convinced his parents to buy it and enter into the hospitality business. They closed on the hotel in late 2004, and Adam set to work on the renovations and restoration for all of 2005. They had their grand opening in February 2006.

AT FIRST, ADAM DISMISSED the various tools that would be missing and then reappear in a totally different place from where he thought he left them. He chalked it up to the stress of the monumental renovation job. As rooms were finished and electrical appliances plugged in, Adam discovered more oddities. He would plug in a television or clock radio, and it would work fine. Later he would discover the item was not working. After he eliminated all the possible electrical malfunctions by checking the wiring, the breaker box, and so on, he would return to the room and the television or clock radio would work perfectly again.

One day, while Adam was working in guest room 203, he heard the jingling of keys out in the hallway. He thought it was his father, but when his father didn't come into the room to say hello, Adam decided to go look for him. He found his father downstairs and asked him, "Pop, were you just upstairs?" His father said, "No." So, Adam went back up to room 203 and continued working. Ten minutes later, Adam heard the keys jingling in the hallway again. This time he stopped what he was doing and listened intently. He heard them go all the way to the end of the hall, which is about ninety feet long. He went to investigate the hall and found no one there.

After a long day of renovating, Adam was cleaning up so he could leave for the night. He was sweeping the stairs that lead to the basement. He started at the top and worked his way down, step by step. He would drag the broom from the left side of the step over to the right. Half way down the stairs, the wall cuts away, and there is only a railing. This opening is what Adam was aiming for to send the dust and dirt over the edge of the step to fall below so he could gather it into a pile and dispose of it once he made it all the way down the steps. He had about a third of the way to go when he heard the sound of someone sweeping after his sweep. It was some type of echo or instant playback of his sweeping. He would drag the broom from left to right and hear the swooshing sound of the broom as he did this. Before he reset the broom to the next step, he heard the swooshing sound even though he didn't have his broom on the next step. Adam tested this with the next couple of steps and each time he heard the sound mimic his sound. He began to feel uncomfortable and decided to leave. He was the only one in the hotel at the time, so he locked up quickly and went home. The next day he arrived to find a dustpan placed strategically at the bottom of the basement stairs. No one had been in the hotel all night, and he knew for a fact he had not placed the dustpan there.

By this time, Adam's suspicions of the place being haunted were solidifying. While working in the basement, he noticed a cold spot. He inspected the windows, and they were closed, so there wasn't a draft. He noticed on several occasions in the basement this cold spot would be there one minute and gone the next. He also grew cognizant of the feeling of someone staring over his shoulder while he was working. Adam wasn't frightened by this feeling of being watched, but he was uncomfortable with it.

One day he placed his .22-caliber nail gun on the old bar in the basement. This is a special nail gun for driving nails into cement. When he went to retrieve the gun, it was gone. He asked his father if he had moved it, and of course the answer was, "No, I thought you had it." A year later the gun was found in the basement at the bottom of a tool box Adam rarely used. I remember Adam showing me this particular nail gun. It's large, certainly not something one would easily misplace.

When Adam showed me the various places where the events he just told me about occurred, I brought along the digital audio recorder and my digital camera. I decided to leave the audio recorder in room 203 on the bed. Adam left the door open to this room to see if the "jailer's keys" sound would be recorded while we continued up to the attic. While heading from the attic to the main floor, Adam explained to me that the hotel had a major fire in 1958. The rear part of the third floor was completely destroyed. After the fire, the hotel sank into a depressive, rundown boarding house.

On the main floor, just past the basement entrance, Adam showed me the room that a woman named Katherine Shoemaker had lived in when the hotel was a boarding house. Katherine died here of natural causes. The room is on the other side of the wall from the hotel office where Adam and I first sat for the interview. He told me that sometimes, while working in the office, he'll hear someone in "Katherine's room" moving stuff around by the sink. When he looks to see who's there, he finds no one. Is Katherine still rooming at the Hotel Belvidere?

Next we went down to the basement. Adam reenacted for me the broom-sweeping-sound incident while coming down the stairs. Normally, I don't like basements. I always get a head rush and generally am ill at ease in them. The Hotel Belvidere's basement, although far from complete, did not generate my typical "basement feelings." I was so taken with the tin work on the walls and the high ceilings that perhaps I really didn't feel like I was in a basement.

Adam told me about the morbid side business once conducted in the basement. Apparently back in the days of hangings at the court house, which is next door, the rope used for the hanging was brought to the bar of the hotel and cut up to be sold off as souvenirs. We went to where the bar was. It now stands in pieces. Adam is going to refinish this bar and reassemble it. It is a huge wood-carved bar with columns, mirror, and brass rail, and it's absolutely gorgeous.

The basement is gigantic. Adam plans to open a bar and restaurant down there. There is an entrance from the street directly to the basement and plenty of space for a kitchen, private dining or party room, bar, and a restaurant. At present, the Hotel Belvidere does not have a kitchen, and therefore corporate events, meetings, and guests wanting room service rely on local caterers or restaurant delivery.

We went to the far back of the basement where Adam pointed out the exit that was sealed up with bricks. This exit would have brought a person right to the parking lot of the hotel. There was a huge limestone prep sink and the alcove indicating where the brick oven once stood. The hotel did have a kitchen in the basement at one time. I was taking pictures but didn't notice anything paranormal in them.

We concluded the tour, and I went back to room 203 to retrieve my digital recorder. Before I left, Adam agreed to have the NJGHS conduct a formal investigation of the hotel. I couldn't wait to get home and review the recordings and the pictures. Although nothing paranormal was evident in the photos or audio recordings, I had that feeling that it was still worth an investigation. I e-mailed NJGHS members Dina Chirico, Brian Sandt, Dave Rountree, and Elaine Macula to see whether they could be part of the team to investigate. Dave had a schedule conflict, so the team consisted of Dina, Brian, Elaine, and me. We coordinated with Adam to investigate on March 2 from 8:00 to 10:00 p.m.

It was a perfectly clear night when we arrived. The moon was waning and would be new in a few days. Adam met us and took us to the third floor, where he set aside a guest suite for us to use as our home base. I was able to brief the team ahead of time about Adam's experiences. This saved us time, and we went right to testing our equipment and loading fresh batteries. I took inventory of the equipment and decided what camcorders would go where on tripods and which ones would be carried around. Elaine set up her camcorder in the attic. Brian set up his in the basement, directed to where Adam said he felt the cold spot. Dina placed her digital audio recorder in room 203. I carried my equipment with me to switch between pieces depending on the location.

A side note for ghost hunters: I discovered that a fishing vest is the best thing to have in your ghost hunting gear. It holds everything. I got mine at Wal-Mart for $15. It has a clip for the thermal scanner and pockets galore to hold batteries, camera, digital audio recorder, and anything else you might need to keep handy. The NJGHS took it a step farther by printing out our logo on iron transfers and personalizing the backs of the vests.

Adam took all of us to the section of the hotel that I didn't see the day I was there. This is another huge area that could serve as a wedding hall once it's renovated. We didn't capture anything paranormal here. After this, we went back into the hotel, and Adam said he would be watching TV with his wife in Katherine's old room and that we could call him on the house phone when we were ready to leave.

While all four of us were on the landing of the third floor, I took a picture looking down the stairs toward the door on the second floor. I got an orb right in the doorway. Dina, who was standing beside me, took a picture immediately after and she captured the same orb but in a different area of the doorway. When I took my next picture, no orb was there.

We split up for a bit with Dina and Elaine in the attic and Brian and me in the basement. We wrapped up just shortly after 10 o'clock. I advised Adam that we would have to review the data and let him know whether we found anything. He was open to the idea of a team coming back for an all-night investigation when there wouldn't be any paying guests staying at the hotel. This would allow us to turn all the lights out.

About two weeks later, I finished compiling the Report of Findings from everyone's data and sent it off to Adam. Dina captured an impressive EVP with her digital audio recorder in the lobby of the hotel, a female voice that says, "Look at the wolf." There is an odd screeching sound at the conclusion of the word "wolf" too. Elaine had an EVP of a little girl's voice saying something we couldn't understand and a baby's laugh. While Dina was in Katherine's room, she said Katherine's last name, Shoemaker, incorrectly on purpose. She recorded an EVP of a female's voice correctly pronouncing the surname. There were seven total EVPs.

Brian and I did not capture any EVPs. I did have the orb photo, but that was it for my results. Elaine captured a bizarre image of a flame in the attic with her video camera. The camera was pointing toward the Front Street side of the building. It appears as a little spark of light and then grows into a flame and vanishes. We still don't know what to make of this. I wondered if it was related to the 1958 fire.

I feel the evidence we collected combined with Adam's experiences demonstrates there is paranormal activity at the Hotel Belvidere, but I look forward to doing the overnight investigation Adam offered. In the meantime, pack your bags: next stop, the Hotel Belvidere.

CHAPTER 27

Harry's Road House
ASBURY PARK

IN DECEMBER 2002, HARRY'S ROAD HOUSE opened for business in the depressed downtown of Asbury Park. Since that time, and through much local effort, the district has undergone a resurgence of businesses for dining and shopping. The old Harry's, at 662 Cookman Avenue, is now a Greek and Mediterranean restaurant called Synaxis at the Shore.

The public relations manager at Harry's, Una, first contacted me in July 2003. Her e-mail explained that she feared the restaurant was haunted. She had had an experience when locking her office door one night, and other employees had encounters as well.

The first time I arrived to investigate Harry's was on a Saturday night. Business was in full swing, so needless to say, it was very loud with the live band playing in the bar. Una took me and my fiancé at the time, Stephen, to a separate dining room that was closed for the night so we could hear ourselves think. I took out my trusty digital audio recorder and questionnaire to document the basics while interviewing her. Una told me that she is sensitive to otherworldly things. I found her to be a grounded, gifted event coordinator and promoter as she showed me the various posters for upcoming events she had planned and designed.

Una described her major experience with this ghost. After working late, she was locking the door to her office, in the basement. When she pushed the door shut to turn the key, it pushed back. She said the force was direct and obvious. She took a second to make sure someone was not on the other side pushing the door to get out, but then she remembered she had been the only one in the office. She decided to push with greater force and hold the door shut while she turned the key to lock the office door. Once she did, she said she was overcome with complete sadness. She said she felt like she was ready to cry, and yet for no apparent reason. The unaccountable sadness just came over her so intensely. Then she heard in her head the words, "I shouldn't have been here," repeatedly.

Una heard reports from other female shift managers about customers coming to them to say they heard a woman crying in the ladies restroom. The female manager would enter the restroom to see if this person needed help, only to find no one there. Una heard from the garbage man that when he was collecting the trash one morning around 4:00 a.m., he heard a woman's voice call him by name. He didn't see anyone and therefore did not answer. Una was convinced they had a ghost in the restaurant, but she couldn't persuade her general manager, Andrew, to let her contact the NJGHS for an investigation.

One night, Andrew was in the basement with two chefs after the restaurant was closed. They were taking inventory and setting up menu selections for the next day. Finally, they were ready to call it a night and head upstairs. As they made their way to the stairs, Andrew noticed a woman standing at the end of the basement in front of Una's office door. Andrew called to the woman to advise her that the restaurant was closed and she needed to leave. She did not respond. He said he took a couple steps toward her and said, "Excuse me, ma'am, we're closed. You need to leave." With that, she vanished right in front of him. He turned around to ask the chefs if they had seen her too, but they were already up the stairs. The next day he told Una, "Call those ghost hunting people. Get them in here."

After I finished interviewing Una and speaking with Andrew about his experience with this ghost, I did a walk-through with Una. I felt a little odd making my way through the crowd in the bar with "ghost hunter geek gear" in hand. I certainly got some inquisitive stares.

We went down the stairs to the ladies' room where the female crying ghost had been heard by several patrons. I took some pictures and EMF readings and scanned for the ambient temperature with the thermal scanner. Una showed me the particular stall where women had heard the crying. At this point, all I could hear was the band blaring away upstairs. None of the equipment I was using picked up any anomalies.

We then went down the back stairs to the basement. Una showed me her office and demonstrated the way the door pushed back at her the night she experienced the sadness and the words in her head. I couldn't do any EVP collection in the basement because of the loud compressors and fans running on the many industrial-strength freezers and refrigerators. Also, the exhaust from these refrigerators and freezers was hot enough that it threw off the thermal scanner readings considerably. I asked Una whether we could turn the lights out in this section by her office. She did turn the lights off, and at that point I was at the mercy of the light emanating from my digital camera. I began to take pictures while carefully moving around the back half of the basement. I did get an orb in the room off to the right of Una's office. It did not appear in the subsequent pictures I took in the same area. Aside from this one photo anomaly, there was nothing to indicate paranormal activity.

We decided it would be best to come back when the restaurant was closed to work more on collecting EVPs. A couple weeks later we returned at 2:00 a.m. The band that had played that night was packing up, and all the patrons had left the building. There were a few employees on hand to clean and reset the place for the next day. Una greeted us and let us use the one booth in the dining room that was clear as our "base camp." Stephen was going to take pictures while I conducted the EVP work. I also had my thermal scanner handy.

We went to the basement again by Una's office. I found that by being in this area, I was farther away from the sounds of the freezers and refrigerators. I asked simple questions like, "Can you tell me your name?" "What do you want me to know?" I wandered in and out of the darkness in this area of the basement for approximately forty-five minutes trying to collect EVPs. I wasn't successful. However, Steve was tracking a particular orb while taking digital pictures.

Again I investigated the ladies' room and tried, with substantially more quiet now, to collect EVPs. I did not hear any voice other than my own upon playback. It can be very frustrating to hear all these stories and experiences and show up to investigate and get nothing in the way of evidence to support them. By 4:00 a.m., my frustration and exhaustion had dampened my enthusiasm, and we called it a night.

Driving home, Stephen said to me that he would take some

of his upcoming vacation time to do historical research on the building and the area. Since he's a history teacher, and history was a subject that bored me to tears in school, I was more than glad to have him do the research.

Steve went to the Asbury Park Library the following week. He asked the reference librarian whether she had any murder or crime case information dating back about a hundred years. She directed him to review the sewer and tax maps to determine when the building in question was constructed. Feeling like he was getting nowhere, he decided he would head to the Monmouth County Library to conduct the research. As he was about to get into his truck, an old man approached him and asked Steve if he was a cop. Apparently this old man and his friend were seated at a table inside the library and overheard Steve's questions to the reference librarian. The old man was concerned that Steve was looking into the political issues that were brewing in Asbury Park. Steve told him that he was merely doing research for an author, figuring the old man would be more forthcoming hearing this rather than it was related to a ghost investigation. The old man told Steve to look up the murder of Marie Smith in 1910.

Steve went back into the library and reviewed the sewer and tax maps for 1910. There was no building at 662 Cookman Avenue at that time. It was an open area with a building a little farther up the street that was called the Youth Center. The building that housed Harry's wasn't constructed until sometime in the 1930s.

Steve headed to the county library and its comprehensive collection of microfiche. While there, he searched the Internet and found a book and movie that detailed Marie Smith's murder.

Marie Smith was a nine-year-old student of the Bradley School in Asbury Park. She lived in the Whitesville section of Neptune and walked a mile to and from school each day. On a cold November day, she was to come home from school by 11:00

a.m. and have her lunch and then deliver her father his lunch at work on her way back to school. By 2:30, she had not come home, and her mother was worried as it was out of character for Marie to disobey. Her mother went to Marie's school and learned from her teacher that Marie did in fact leave school at recess at 10:30.

Sadly, Marie's mutilated body was found on November 15, 1910, approximately 150 yards from where the restaurant is today, in a wooded area bordering Deal Lake. The town was in an uproar over the murder of this little girl. A black handyman named Thomas Williams who was seen in the neighborhood and had a criminal record was arrested. He was beaten severely in jail in an attempt to get him to confess to her murder. He maintained his innocence, and the newly formed National Association for the Advancement of Colored People secured his release.

The sheriff hired private investigator Raymond C. Schindler, who went undercover as a credit investigator and canvassed the neighborhood around Marie's home and school. He came across twenty-seven-year-old Frank Heideman, a German immigrant who worked for the Kruschka Florist and lived in a house owned by the florist. The floral shop was near Marie's school. Heideman had a criminal record for child molestation back in Germany. Schindler was convinced he had his prime suspect. He conducted an elaborate sting operation by planting an undercover officer to befriend Heideman and gain his trust to elicit a confession. It worked, and Heideman confessed to Marie Smith's murder. Approximately four weeks after Heideman's trial, in which he pleaded not-guilty in spite of his written and signed confession to the contrary, he was put to death in the electric chair, on May 23, 1911.

The pieces of our ghost investigation were coming together. The ghost heard crying in the bathroom, seen in the basement, and heard outside by the trash collector could be Marie Smith's grief-stricken mother. Perhaps she watches over the area where her daughter tragically met her demise. With further research we learned that the Youth Center was a clothing store in 1910. From the name, we had thought it was a YMCA-type of place where kids congregated for after-school programs. Steve realized from the sewer maps that Bradley School was across town from the Youth Center. While reading through some of the clips of the reports from the time, I learned that Marie had worn a coat that was too small for her. She was one of three children with a fourth on the way, and with only one income in the family, it stands to reason that she may not have had a wide selection of well-fitting, fashionable clothing. It's possible that Heideman had offered to take the little girl clothes shopping and instead molested and murdered her in the woods near this store. Clearly, Marie should not have been in this area. This realization in effect explains the words that Una heard in her head.

While I was visiting Asbury Park in 2008 to take some pictures for this book, I stopped by a neat store specializing in retro reproductions of kitchenware and collectibles called Flying Saucers. This store is in the lower level of "the arcade," which used to be a Woolworth's. I spoke with the store owner, James Kaufman, and asked about Harry's Road House. "That was two restaurants ago," he said. "Now it's a Greek restaurant." I confessed that I was working on my ghost hunting book, and he said he had heard stories of the place being haunted but never experienced anything first hand. Of course, I couldn't leave empty handed, so I bought cool little refrigerator magnets of concert posters for the Doors, the Ramones, and the Monkees.

I was exiting the arcade when a gentleman named Don Stine asked whether I was the lady inquiring about the ghosts at Harry's. He said he had owned and operated his bookstore for years at 721 Cookman Avenue and that he had heard various stories from people who worked at Harry's about the ghost of a ten-year-old girl with long dark hair. This would not fit the description of Marie Smith, however, who was described as small for her age with short sandy hair.

Don told me about some other incidents that must have happened well after I investigated Harry's. He flat out told the manager who was hired to replace Andrew, "You know the place is haunted, right?" The manager, who was Hispanic, concurred. He added that he already had some encounters to make him a believer. Don said that one morning when the new manager arrived to open for the day's business, he found every burner on the stove lit at full blast. It's a wonder the place didn't burn down. Interesting to note, Don also said there was a fire in this building's history and that is why there is no second floor. After that fire, they just rebuilt the first floor. Don thinks the ghost girl that people witness may be a victim of that fire. This was the first I had heard of the fire and admit more research on my part would be in order to make any such conclusions.

At the end of the day, it doesn't seem to matter what the menu is at 662 Cookman Avenue in Asbury Park. Whether it's a road house or Greek restaurant, there's a side order of paranormal with every entrée.

CHAPTER 28

Bus Crash Ghosts

CHEESEQUAKE

THE GARDEN STATE PARKWAY IS 173 MILES
LONG. It has 359 exits and entrances, which account for the
running joke of, "You're from Jersey? What exit?" The first toll
section opened on January 15, 1954, and the entire parkway was
completed July 1, 1955. It stretches the length of New Jersey
from Montvale, near the New York border, to Cape May Ferry.
Along these miles of highway, there are many stories of ghostly
encounters. I personally investigated one of them.

It was a bitter-cold Christmas Eve day in 1998. A bus from
the Bruin Transportation Company in Brooklyn, New York, was

making its way down the Garden State Parkway to Atlantic City carrying mostly senior citizens for a day trip to the casinos. The road was slick, given the one to two inches of snow that had fallen the night before. The bus was rumbling south on the parkway uneventfully when the driver lost control of the vehicle and it began to slide. It crashed through the guardrail, flipped on its side, and landed on the embankment by the Cheesequake rest stop between exits 123 and 124.

It was 11:00 a.m., and employees at the rest stop were almost finished with their shift and ready to go home for Christmas festivities. Upon hearing the crash, they scrambled to grab blankets and tools and make their way to the crash scene to help the injured. Bodies were pinned beneath the wreckage. Other people were trapped within the bus and waiting for rescuers to free them.

News reporter Alan David Stein was at a press conference in Perth Amboy. He said the conference was getting under way when all the reporters' beepers started going off. It was a mass exodus to head to the scene of the bus crash. When Alan arrived at the scene he said, "It looked like a plane crash. Bodies were everywhere covered in white sheets."

Eight people were confirmed dead on the scene, and twenty-two people were injured, with several evacuated by helicopter. The next day, makeshift memorials were in place near the scene for those who died in the crash. The bus had been moved to a garage for examination. Alan said the bus was "horribly mangled." The accident was later determined to be a combination of mechanical problems and the ice on the roadway.

In early October of 2000, Alan, then working as a reporter for NJ 101.5-FM, contacted me about a Halloween feature story he was working on. He said it would be called "Ghost Jersey." The week of Halloween, a segment would air each morning Monday through Friday during the *Jim Gerhardt Show*. He wanted to know whether I could provide him with some haunted hot spots for his segments as well as general information about ghost hunting. I mentioned Spy House to him, and he reminded me about the bus crash. I vaguely recalled the crash as I'm not one to watch the news. He and I discussed a time to meet to travel to the Spy House and the bus crash scene.

Alan got his first ride in a classic hearse the night we met to scope out the two sites. "Baby" was my 1974 hunter-green Miller-Meteor Cadillac hearse complete with a poor boy casket in the back. Honestly, the hearses today are so sleek and pretty. "Baby" was twenty-two feet of morbid foreboding.

At the Cheesequake rest area, Alan directed me to pull the car off the road and park it on the shoulder of the on-off ramp. With flashlights and digital camera in hand, we made our way to a grassy slope where the fatal bus crash had taken place almost two years prior. Alan pointed the beam of his flashlight on the spot where the covered bodies had been laid. Meanwhile, I kept taking pictures. Back then I had a new Sony Mavica that had 1 megapixel resolution and stored images on a 3.5" floppy disk. I wasn't getting any pictures worth writing home about, but I kept taking them. Finally, a huge orb appeared in the shot. I immediately took another picture and the orb was gone. This was a clear and cool October night. I can attest that there were no bugs, moisture, or pollen to account for this one brilliant orb. I scrolled back on the view screen to show Alan the image. He had never seen an orb before.

No other findings were documented at this location. The temperature remained constant, and no EMF readings were detected.

Alan said he always wondered, given the tragedy of this crash, if the area would be marked with a haunting. I figured it might be a residual haunting wherein the sounds of the crash

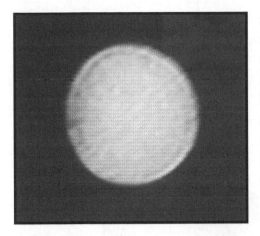

Large orb from the Garden State Parkway bus crash

replay. Then again, there might be an earth-bound soul or two that linger at the site of the crash because they are confused and don't realize they're dead. They may be stuck in that scene and only see the crash and the rescue workers covering victims' bodies, but don't realize it's their bodies.

The "Ghost Jersey" radio series aired and was simulcast on Comcast cable television's CN8 each morning the week of Halloween. I was able to videotape the segments for posterity. Sadly, that is the only record I have of that gorgeous orb. Much of my early research and floppies were casualties of the "Great Hot Water Heater Flood of 2001." Yes, my office was in the basement right by the ill-fated hot water heater. I tried to take a picture of the orb from the shaky video footage, and I've included it in this book, but it certainly doesn't do the original justice.

Today Alan has his own talk show on WCTC 1450-AM in Somerset. I was on his show for Halloween in 2007. While he loved the latest ghost-investigation tales I shared, he still remembers the ride in the hearse most fondly.

As for the bus crash scene, I haven't been back to investigate it. The space is not easy to navigate in terms of parking your vehicle. For some, Cheesequake is a great rest area to visit when making the late-night journey home from the Jersey Shore. For others, it is their final rest stop.

CHAPTER 29

The Ghost of Baltus Roll

SPRINGFIELD

MANY PEOPLE KNOW WASHINGTON IRVING'S CLASSIC "The Legend of Sleepy Hollow" with its headless horseman. While Irving's tale takes place in the Hudson Valley of New York state, the event he based it on took place in New Jersey. The Great Swamp is where the Hessian soldier had his head blown off by a cannon ball during the Revolutionary War. (Hessians were conscripted German soldiers who fought for the British.) Headless ghosts are said to be the most violent and frightening because beheading is so traumatic and sudden. The victim's last emotional experience is one of intense anger and rage over the incident. The earthbound, headless spirit is on a vengeful path to recoup his head and inflict his wrath upon anyone who dares get in his way.

I heard for years that there was a headless ghost upon his steed charging up Summit Road in the Watchung Reservation, but the closest I came to experiencing such a heart-pounding event was when I was driving home from work one night. As I made the right turn onto Summit Avenue, I saw a horse with no rider coming straight at me. Fortunately there was no oncoming car in the opposite lane, so I was able to swerve to avoid hitting the horse. I quickly got back on course in my lane. I wasn't sure what to do, but the thought of that horse making its way to the intersection scared me. Just then I saw a woman on a horse charging up the street from the Watchung Stables with lasso ready in hand. I was slowly continuing down the road and watching in the rear view mirror to see the event unfold. They disappeared from my view as I was farther down the slope in the road. I read in the newspaper that the woman on horseback was able to catch the errant horse and bring him back to the stable.

As for a headless horseman in the Watchung Reservation, I have not witnessed one, and I have not found any documentation of one. However, there is a ghost who roams the mountaintop in the Watchung Reservation as well as the fairways of the Galloping Hill Golf Course in Kenilworth. It is suspected to be the ghost of Baltus Roll.

Baltus Roll, born in 1769, was the grandson of Johnnes Roll, a Dutch pioneer who settled in the Westfield area in 1740. Baltus was a farmer and trader who lived with his wife in a simple home. They did not have any children.

On February 22, 1831, Baltus and his wife went to bed early. Around midnight, two men pounded on the front door and Baltus refused to let them in. They forced their way into the home and captured Baltus. They beat him and dragged him outside. The larger of the two men told Baltus' wife to stay in bed. She snuck out of bed and went downstairs to see the two men brutally beating her husband and tossing him in an icy puddle of water. Baltus called twice to his wife. Thinking Baltus was dead, his wife made her escape. She trudged through the woods in the snow and rain till morning, when she returned home to see the lifeless body of Baltus in the snow. Rather than risk going into her home to find the murderers still there, she went to the neighbor's house and asked for their help.

Jesse Cahoon, Brook Sayre, and Joseph Cain went back to the Roll house with Mrs. Roll. They found Baltus naked, bound by rope at his hands and feet, and lying dead by the gate. The house had been completely ransacked. The coroner determined the cause of death was strangulation, given the finger marks on Baltus' throat.

Two men were suspected in the murder: Peter Davis and Lycidias Baldwin. It was common knowledge that Davis needed money. He had recruited Baldwin to help him rob the Rolls since it was rumored that Baltus hid a large sum of money in his home. Davis was arrested, and Baldwin fled to Morristown only to commit suicide later in a tavern there.

Eventually Davis was acquitted because the damaging testimony was ruled "illegal." However, he pleaded guilty to three of the four indictments of forgery and was sentenced to thirty-two years in prison, where he eventually died.

Baltus Roll's grave is in the Presbyterian Church cemetery on Mountain Avenue in Westfield. I believe his widow wanted everyone to know that her husband was murdered despite the acquittal and had the word "murdered" inscribed on Baltus' gravestone rather than "died." Additionally, she had the following words put on his gravestone: "Ye friends that weep around my grave. Compose your minds to rest. Prepare with me for sudden death and live forever blest."

Baltus's ghost has been seen at the Galloping Hills Golf

Galloping Hills Golf Course

Course, which is odd because it's in Kenilworth and the golf course that bears his name is in Springfield. Baltusrol Country Club is made up of the very land that Baltus once farmed. So why does he haunt the public golf course? This could be explained by confusion the spirit has over his death and how the landscape has changed since 1831. Also, Galloping Hills Golf Course sits between two cemeteries: Graceland Memorial Park and Beth David Cemetery. Perhaps these final resting places have a magnetic pull for Baltus.

In 1999 the NJGHS investigated the Presbyterian Church cemetery in Westfield. I was still using a 35mm camera at the time. Although the cemetery is small and one block up from the movie theater and the center of town, we were able to capture some results. I did have a great orb picture from this investigation. I don't have the print of this photo any longer since I lost many files when my basement flooded. However, there is a thumbnail of it on the Internet Archive Wayback Machine: http://web.archive.org/web/*/http://njghs.net. Click on "March 2, 2000," and then scroll near the bottom of the page and click on the "Ghost Photos link." The photo is named "PCC Cemetery." I don't recall any of the other investigators securing EVP. We were there on a Friday night, so it was very noisy in town.

I do have a great ghost encounter for the Presbyterian Church cemetery that happened about fifteen years ago. It almost sounds too good to be true, but given that the man who relayed this story to me is a police officer in town, I trust its accuracy. The officer told me his friends' eyewitness account of a full-body apparition. He said his friends were walking down Mountain Avenue toward the center of town late one night. The two women were talking when they heard the snorting sound of a horse. When they stopped talking and looked up at the gate, they saw a figure of a man on his horse. The horse reared up, and then the apparition charged off into the darkness of the cemetery and vanished from sight. The two women were terrified by what they experienced. From a ghost hunter's perspective, that's the best part of the story—not that they were terrified, but that they both saw and heard it.

The next day one of the women called the officer to tell him what happened to her and her friend the night before. She wanted to know if he ever got any reports of such sightings. Even though he had never had any reports like this before, he said he trusted they would not make something like this up. Plus, he said judging from how shaken they were the day after, he sensed their sincerity in the event.

Perhaps the ghost of Baltus Roll rides again in the afterlife seeking justice for his murder. Or, at the very least, he roams the Watchung Mountains and ruins a good game of golf in Kenilworth.

CHAPTER 30

The Proprietary House
PERTH AMBOY

THE PROPRIETARY HOUSE WAS THE NAME GIVEN
to this structure built by the Proprietors of East New Jersey.
Located in Perth Amboy, it was completed in 1764 and inhabited by the Royal Governor William Franklin, son of Benjamin
Franklin, and his wife of two years. Although Benjamin urged
William to forsake his loyalty to the British crown, William
refused. He was arrested and removed from the palace in 1776.

Post-Revolutionary War, the Proprietary House suffered
damage from a fire. John Rattoon bought the property in 1794
and began to repair the building. In 1808, Rattoon sold it to Richard Woodhull, who converted it to a hotel called the Brighton.

Woodhull constructed a three-story addition and a two-story porch, also adding other structural enhancements.

The War of 1812 brought more damage to the Proprietary House, and it was sold in a sheriff's sale to Mathias Bruen in 1817. Bruen tried to resurrect the Brighton Hotel over several decades, but the economy would not bear it, given the Mexican and Civil wars. Bruen conveyed the Proprietary House to the Presbyterian Board of Relief for Disabled Ministers and the Wives and Orphans of Deceased Ministers in 1883, and it became known as the Westminster. By 1903, the Proprietary House was returned to the Bruen family, which sold it in 1904.

The new owners turned it into a nice apartment building with a public restaurant, but it again fell into disrepair and became a rooming house. By 1966 the Proprietary House Association had taken over the maintenance of the property for the state of New Jersey. After ten years of restorative work, the first two floors of the building were opened to the public. Sadly, further deterioration of the building outpaced the restoration. In 1986 the Restoration Partnership of Boston agreed to lease the house and three and a half acres of surrounding land for twenty-five years. The partnership also agreed to restore and renovate the exterior as well as finish the interior of the 1809 wing. Income drawn from the restored offices on the upper floors would reimburse the partnership. Today the Proprietary House Association leases the first two floors from the state of New Jersey and conducts various events to raise the money necessary to pay the lease.

By the time the NJGHS got to investigate the Proprietary House, on April 28, 2006, it appeared to be in a controlled state of disrepair. I could see the inherent beauty in the structure. It's truly a shame that funding is inadequate to restore it to its early grandeur.

It was a cool but humid night when we investigated. The NJGHS team consisted of Dina Chirico, Gregory and Sherry

Irish, Laura Lindemann, Dawn Eastmed, Laci Williams, Brian Sandt, and me. A volunteer from the Proprietary House Association was there to let us in and take us on a tour of the house. She explained the history of the house and then led us to the main ballroom or living room that was set with round tables and chairs for an upcoming event that weekend. I believe it was to be someone's bridal shower, but I don't remember for certain. In this large room, she showed us the elevator and said that psychic Jane Doherty has seen a little boy ghost in this area.

We went down to the basement. The wine cellar room is where the association holds its Wednesday-afternoon high teas. This room is shaped like a rainbow in that there are no walls forming ninety-degree angles with the ceiling. It's an arc shape. Jane saw a Revolutionary War soldier, in full uniform, standing just outside this room. She watched him turn and walk through the wall. She included this information on her ghost tours, and the newspapers printed the story. That is what brought a gentleman forward who saw the same apparition forty years ago while he was working on renovations for the Proprietary House. When I spoke with Jane about this room and its tunnel shape, she said that it is rumored there were tunnels that led to the waterfront.

We continued to tour the basement by viewing the kitchen and the ladies' room. The volunteer said that the kitchen was rather quiet in terms of paranormal activity, but the ladies' room was another story. She said women have been locked in the restroom by unseen hands.

We were not allowed to investigate on the third floor because of the various business offices there. The doors to those offices were locked as well. We returned to the main floor and split into smaller teams to cover the large space.

Brian and I went back to the wine cellar. Brian set up his camcorder on a tripod just inside the doorway of this room pointing toward the wall where the soldier has been seen standing and walking. In the opposite corner of the room, he placed a large black light to aid the infrared recording of the camcorder. Brian told me that black lights work like floodlights for infrared. He was right. It looks strange to the naked eye, but when I looked through the camera lens, it appeared as if the whole room was illuminated perfectly for infrared. Brian had to warn me and anyone else who came into this room to not use a flash while taking a picture as it would be damaging to his camcorder in this recording mode.

I took some digital still pictures, without the flash, in this room. I did not record any orbs or paranormal anomalies. The temperature was constant, around sixty-five degrees. I used my digital camcorder to take pictures in its NightShot mode but failed to capture any paranormal activity as well. The night was young, so I figured it best to leave the room and let the equipment record on its own. Brian and I went back upstairs.

Dina was investigating the large ballroom. She showed me the orb pictures she had captured. I thought they were interesting and took a couple of pictures myself in the same area, but did not capture any orbs. Gregory and Sherry were investigating the entrance and front room while Laci and Dawn were on the second floor. Gregory captured an orb picture in the front room where we first convened and stored our coats and bags. We were all taking our time, and whispering if we spoke at all, to allow for EVP recordings.

I decided to go back downstairs and sit in the tea room and record for EVP. Sherry opted to join me. When we entered the room, we looked to see whether any of the chairs or tea cups had been moved. It's reported that on occasion the volunteers will find two chairs pulled back from a table and the teacups right side up as if someone had been having tea and conversation. All the teacups were inverted on their saucers and the chairs were in place by each table. Sherry and I sat at the second table in on

Orb captured in a photo taken by Gregory Irish at the Proprietary House

the right, close to where the soldier is seen to walk through the wall. I turned my digital audio recorder on and said, "If there is anyone here who would like to tell us your name or your story, please do." We sat there quietly observing the room. After about ten minutes, I stopped the recorder and played back the recording to review it. As we were listening, Brian and Gregory came downstairs. I stopped the recorder and reset it to a new folder to record in. Brian needed to change the DVD in his camcorder. Gregory took some EMF readings of the room, which were all normal.

I had to use the ladies' room and admitted my apprehension aloud. Thankfully, Sherry is gifted with "bladder empathy" and went with me. I was tempted to bring the audio recorder with me, but negated the idea. It would be my luck to capture the best EVP ever and have the tape circulate widely.

We joined the rest of the crew on the main floor. We had been investigating for more than an hour with minimal immediate results. I was hopeful that the camcorder had recorded something when we left the room, but we wouldn't know for sure until the next day when Brian reviewed the recording.

We continued a little while longer to pace through the house on the various floors and take pictures and recordings. Finally, I made friends with a folding chair in the ballroom by the door to the elevator. Sherry, Laura L., and Dina came in and sat down too. We were discussing how this was anticlimactic considering all we'd heard about how haunted the place is. I told them how the ghost boy is "seen" by the doorway I was sitting next to. I jokingly put my hand up to high-five the ghost boy, and Dina took a picture. It would have been exceedingly cool had the boy's full-body apparition been in the picture "high-fiving" me back, but that didn't happen. It's just a picture of me strengthening the consensus as to what an idiot I am.

Laci and Dawn came in the room and said they were beat. We decided to wrap up the investigation and pack up our equipment. We agreed to share any findings after reviewing the data over the next couple of days.

Other than the orb shots that Dina and Gregory captured, nothing else was noted for paranormal activity. Brian reviewed all his video footage and saw nothing out of the ordinary. I think we just hit the Proprietary House on a slow night. I believe it to be actively haunted given the experiences Jane Doherty has had while conducting her séances and ghost tours there. She's spent a lot more time there than I have.

I spoke with Jane about her experiences. She told me about the footsteps heard during one of her séances. A Proprietary House trustee on duty thought someone from Jane's séance was walking in the hallway. Jane and the séance attendees thought the footsteps were that of the trustee. When they later compared notes, Jane and the trustee realized the footsteps were neither of theirs.

Disembodied footsteps are a step above an orb picture (pardon the pun). It gets better. Jane told me two years ago that while conducting the ghost tours she felt she was touched upstairs in the far corner near the breakfast room that Franklin used. She said it was a light-pressure sensation just below her waist. As the night wore on, the pressure or strength of the touch in that same location increased with each tour she brought up there. She wondered what would happen by the time of the last tour, but nothing beyond the touch manifested. She did sense the presence to be that of a man.

Jane shares the story about the ghost boy on her tours. She has seen this ghost boy and describes him as wearing knickers, and his outfit is predominantly blue in color. Given the history of the Proprietary House, it's possible this may be the ghost of a boy from when the building was used as a home for reverends' widows and their children or perhaps when it was an orphanage. Jane psychically detects that this boy died by falling out of a window, or he was pushed out a window to his death. This ghost boy manifests so fully that Proprietary House neighbors have seen him knocking on the front door to gain entrance or playing in their yards or in the neighborhood in general. Neighbors wonder where he lives and why he is dressed in such funny clothes.

The best example of this ghost boy manifesting that Jane shared with me happened a couple of years ago. There are offices rented out on the third floor of the Proprietary House. One of the tenants had to spend the night in his office waiting on the delivery of an important package via courier. Around 5:00 a.m., the courier arrived at the Proprietary House. The boy unlocked the front door and waved the courier in. The boy led the courier to the elevator and rode with him to the third floor. When the elevator door opened, the courier went to the office to deliver the package, and the boy went in the opposite direction. The gentleman in the office awoke when the courier walked in and said, "How did you get in here?" The courier replied, "Your son let me in."

I'm sure when the worker explained that he didn't have his son with him at the office, there was a very quick "Sign here please," and they both scrambled for the exit.

Unfortunately for me, as a ghost hunter, I did not experience any of these apparitions while investigating the Proprietary House. Then again, I'm glad I didn't experience the horse-manure smell that people have noted while having their tea in the wine cellar. This is a residual haunting of when horses and other farm animals were hidden in the basement to prevent them from being stolen. I doubt there is an air freshening product on the market for paranormal odor. I would recommend braving the potential smell for a cup of tea at the Proprietary House, or better still, take one of Jane Doherty's ghost tours.

CHAPTER 31

Liquid Assets

SOUTH PLAINFIELD

"CHECK OUT THE ORBS ON THAT!"

"Now that's a full-body apparition!"

Okay, let's get the sexual innuendos out of the way right now. Yes, Liquid Assets is a gentlemen's club in South Plainfield. I've been to haunted castles, cemeteries, bed and breakfasts, and restaurants and even trekked in ankle-deep snow around a former asylum, but this was truly uncharted territory for me. Pushing aside my personal objections to this type of business, I ventured into the bar to interview John Colasanti, the owner.

It was 1:30 p.m. when I arrived on a cloudy day in March 2008. Yet it looked like 1:30 a.m. inside this place. I've never been to such a place, so I'm assuming they're all kept dark like that. I have no idea. I'm sure I stood out like a sore thumb, being female and fully clothed, so it didn't take long for a young man to ask if he could help me. I told him I had an appointment with John, and he said he would let him know I was there. He vanished through a door and left me standing there in that uncomfortable space. John came out to greet me within minutes. I put my hand out to shake his and he took my hand but pulled me in for a nice hug hello. I'm used to conducting business with a handshake and a smile, so this was yet another uncomfortable and awkward moment for me. I suppose in this flesh-on-display business, formalities are dispensed with and everyone is referred to as "sweetheart." In my corporate mindset, I would never allow anyone at work to refer to me as "sweetie" or "honey," but this was his turf, and I had to assimilate only enough to get through the interview. At least that is what I kept repeating in my head.

John is a nice guy. I have to say that. We went into his office and sat down in front of the computer. This computer is part of the security system. There are cameras mounted on the outside

John Colasant, owner of Liquid Assets

of the building to monitor the alley and the parking lot. The surveillance footage is available for real-time viewing.

Starting in July 2002, John witnessed and recorded a ghostly anomaly on these surveillance cameras in the parking lot and alley. I reviewed these film clips on Jane Doherty's Web site (http://www.janedoherty.com) prior to my meeting with John. Plus, I made it a point to scrutinize the parking lot and alley while I was there that day. I took several pictures of the lot aimed at the telephone pole that appeared to be the center of ghostly attention, as well as of the alley. I didn't see any reflective signs or surfaces on the telephone pole to possibly explain the manifestation.

Additionally, if it were something reflective, it would have been there constantly, or at least in the same section of the screen. This amorphous white shadow had the ability to come and go in various areas. It seemed to exhibit a consciousness in that it would disappear or hide when a person was present and come back out when the person left. For example, one video shows the white shadow moving around the telephone pole and then disappearing when the bread-delivery truck pulls into the lot. The delivery man gets out of his truck, makes his delivery, and gets back in his truck. As soon as the truck exits the lot, the white shadow reappears by the telephone pole.

The alley footage was especially intriguing because John's wife, who was closing up one night, saw a shadowy image on the security screen and called John over to look at it. This shadow was hovering around John's car in the alley alongside the Liquid Assets building. John told her to keep an eye on the screen as he left the office to go inspect the alley. His wife could see the shadow ducking out of sight as John entered the alley. John said he didn't see anything or anyone out there. He went back inside to see if it was still visible on the screen. It was. His wife said that as soon as he came back in the building, the shadow reemerged. He was able to see it on the screen again. John was determined to confront whatever this was, so he went back out to the alley. Again, he did not see anything out there. He even went around the fence to make sure it wasn't someone with a flashlight playing a gag on him. Inside the office, his wife could see the shadow retreat into hiding only to emerge once John went back in the building.

As John opened the video files, I had time to look at the old photos and a movie poster he had on the walls of his office. "So who is Joseph Colasanti?" I asked. He replied, "That was my uncle. He was shot and killed by an off-duty policeman in 1929 in the Bronx."

John went on to tell me about his two uncles, Joseph and Jerry. The latter was shot and killed in a bowling alley in the Bronx in 1931 by "Trigger" Mike Coppola. Joseph was "tossing around" a union boss during the Silk Stocking Strike in 1929. An off-duty officer named Quigley saw the "tossing" while on his front porch. He ran inside his house and retrieved his gun and opened fire on Joseph. John said that his uncle and his associates returned fire from their 1928 Cadillac while leaving the scene.

In addition to the "Brothers Colasanti," there was Vincent "Mad Dog" Cole. Vincent was from County Clare in Ireland. He arrived in the United States with his sister and brother and lived on the streets of New York. John's grandmother, Joseph and Jerry's mother, took young Vincent into their home. He learned Italian from being raised in this family and living in an Italian neighborhood in the Bronx.

Vincent earned his nickname of "Mad Dog" by being ruthless and vicious. John said that after his Uncle Jerry was killed in 1931 as part of the Beer Wars, Vincent was enraged and began kidnapping the hierarchy of the Doug Schultz camp. Doug was known as the "Beer Baron of the Bronx." Vincent was shot and killed in a phone booth in 1932. A poster for the 1961 movie *Mad Dog Cole* hangs in John's office. The poster shows what appears to be a strip club from that time period.

Normally, I would just stick to the ghost story, but this

information was not only fascinating, it was also pertinent to the haunting of the club. It turns out that when famous psychic medium Jane Doherty was called in to investigate the club and review the videotapes of the apparition, she picked up the names Vincent and Joseph. She had not seen the movie poster or any of the family photos hanging in John's office when she channeled those names. She got the sense that Vincent and Joseph were doing what they could from the other side to help John and his business on this side. Jane feels these spirits are attached to John and followed him from New York to New Jersey.

Before Liquid Assets, there was another strip bar here called Pellegrino's. The man who managed the bar for nine and a half years was my second ex-husband. He spent time in the paranormal investigating world with me while we were married and was trained on the protocols per the NJGHS. He said he never experienced any paranormal activity the whole time he worked there. This supports Jane's theory that the spirits came with John to help him.

The "parking lot ghost" video was a huge help to the club in terms of publicity. The media attention was amazing. John said he and Jane were on news shows on NBC, ABC, UPN 9, and FOX 5 and in the *Newark Star-Ledger, Home News Tribune*, and *New York Post*. Reuters picked up the story and made it international news. John admits that he could have never afforded that kind of publicity. It truly was a boon to the business. In fact, to this day, the sign on the building reads, "Yes, this bar is haunted." John said he got tired of answering that question from patrons, so he just spelled it out on the sign.

John told me some other interesting haunted experiences that took place in the bar. He said that drinks would be left on the bar and they would evaporate. Just to be clear, these drinks were left well after the bar was closed for the night. No one was around, and the security camera did not record a thirsty employee helping himself.

Pictures of ectoplasmic mist and odd lightning-like streaks of light coming up from the feet of the bar stools have been taken inside the bar. I did see the ectoplasmic mist photo, but not the lightning-streaks photos. I would have to discount the ectoplasmic mist photo because at the time it was taken, smoking was still allowed in bars in New Jersey. If it had been a photo that an NJGHS member took, adhering to the investigative protocols, I would know for sure that it was genuine.

John also said that one night after closing, the bar stools were piled on the bar to make cleaning the floor easier, and unseen hands flung a bar stool from the bar onto the floor. Dancers report feeling their hair pulled and don't see anyone there when they turn to confront the person. A dancer was getting ready to leave and stopped to chat at the bar. She had her car keys in her hand when suddenly she felt a force pull them from her. The keys went flying onto the bar and spilled a customer's drink. She apologized to the patron explaining that she did not throw her keys at him or his drink.

I asked John if the activity is still as frequent as it was from 2002 to 2004. He said that it had slowed considerably after 2004. Business has also slowed for Liquid Assets. John said the last time he saw the white shadow image on the screen was during the Christmas holidays of 2007. He told me how Jane Doherty was trying to see whether there was a pattern or rhythm to the appearances, but she didn't discover one. I suggested paying attention once more to the security screens. Perhaps Vincent and Uncle Joe have withdrawn their energies and are not dancing for the camera anymore because they feel neglected.

Liquid Assets is touted as the premier gentlemen's club in New Jersey. If you're like me, the erotic aspect of the bar won't hold your attention. I can spend hours, however, sitting on my "assets" watching those parking-lot ghost videos.

CHAPTER 32

The Cranbury Inn
CRANBURY

GETTING MARRIED? Want a quiet, romantic dinner for two? Looking for that intimate and cozy atmosphere for your next family gathering? Or are you like me and looking for a haunted place to have dinner? The Cranbury Inn is the answer. Located in Middlesex County on Main Street in the Township of Cranbury, the 230-year-old establishment is on the National Register of Historic Places. Tom and Gay Ingegneri have been the owners since 1992. In 2005, they built a timber-frame reception hall on the site of the barn that burned down in 1902. Now they can cater for wedding receptions with up to two hundred guests.

The inn's origins lie in two taverns, one built in the mid-1700s and the other in the late 1700s. The business was officially established in 1780. Originally the town was called variations of Cranberry, as it was a mill town along Cranberry Creek. Its name changed to Cranbury around 1886 as part of the English tradition of calling a small town or village a "burg" or "bury." In 1800, Peter and Hannah Perrine built their home to adjoin the fronts of the two separate taverns, thereby connecting them. The Cranbury Inn was believed to be part of the Underground Railroad. It also housed the telegraph office and justice of the peace. It was incorporated as the Cranbury Inn in 1920 by Judge Joseph Thomas Wincklhofer and his wife, Mary. They were the last owners to live there. In 1930 Adrian and Marge Van Ravesteyn bought the inn and converted the bedrooms into inn rooms and remodeled the newer tavern. Adrian's good friend Albert Einstein would drink beer and speak German with him in the tap room.

Over the years, the inn has seen many notable guests, from foreign dignitaries to modern-day celebrities such as Brooke Shields, who dined at the inn while attending Princeton University. My fellow "Jersey girl" Susan Sarandon and her husband, Tim Robbins, were here with Meg Ryan and Walter Matthau in the mid-1990s for the filming of *I.Q.*

In November 2001, I was contacted by James Nussbaum, executive producer of the cable show *Digithead*. The premise of the show was "infotainment" centered on computer and digital technology and its place in everyday life. He said he learned about the NJGHS from an article that appeared in the *Daily Record* at Halloween. Jim asked me about the types of technology we used to conduct a ghost hunt. I told him about the digital cameras, audio recorders, camcorders, and, of course, the computer for analysis and storage of data. He suggested meeting to discuss the show and the possible appearance of the NJGHS on the show, so I invited him and his crew to attend our Holiday Open House party in December. This was the perfect opportunity for him to meet me and other members without our having a monthly meeting with business to conduct. Little did I know when he showed up solo that he wanted to gauge my sanity and credibility before he brought in the crew. Jim decided I wasn't an ax murderer or some psycho who claims to channel extra-terrestrials and told the crew it was safe to come over and film some interviews with us.

About a week later, he called me to ask about where we could take him and his crew on a ghost hunt for *Digithead*. I reached out to Gay at the Cranbury Inn to see how open she and Tom might be to the idea. Gay told me that it would have to be after Christmas but before New Year's Eve as those were very busy times for them. She and I settled on Sunday, December 30.

I called Jim back with the date and time. He suggested meeting at my house first and consolidating the crew into two vehicles and following the NJGHS in mine. The "Susie home-maker" in me couldn't resist the opportunity to feed people, so I suggested they come an hour earlier and have dinner first. I threw together two big trays of baked manicotti, some salad and cupcakes and cookies for dessert. This is when Jim got his first brush with my weird Aquarian psychic ability. An HBO rep-resentative who was considering carrying *Digithead* had come along to observe and turned out to be lactose intolerant. I've never given the condition much thought, but as I was running upstairs to retrieve a sweater, I yelled down, "If anyone is lactose intolerant and can't eat the manicotti, I have some turkey and stuffing I can reheat for you." The HBO rep was floored. He hadn't said anything yet, but when I came back down, he asked for the turkey. Jim stood there looking at me with a perplexed expression. I've always categorized this psychic ability as useless since it hasn't generated any winning lottery numbers.

After eating, everyone packed up and journeyed south on the New Jersey Turnpike to exit 8A. We arrived at the Cranbury

Inn just before nine. It was a clear and cold night, with a full moon and a lunar eclipse set to take place later. Gay and Tom were there and showed us to the little dining room off the tap room by the wine cellar/liquor store. They kept this dining room free of patrons so we would have a place to convene and store our coats and equipment.

Once I had fresh batteries loaded in the camera and thermal scanner, Jim wanted to get some introduction footage. Thankfully it took only two takes out on the porch as I was freezing and couldn't wear my coat over my blazer. In television, practicality takes a back seat to vanity.

Closing time neared. Jim and his cameraman filmed an interview with Gay about her feelings on the inn and its ghostly inhabitants. Gay said that she is very comfortable with the ghosts. She considers them her friends. "Staying all night at the inn would be like having a slumber party with my friends," she said.

Finally, the last customer left the bar, and the inn officially closed for the night. It was time to investigate. Chip King, the host of the show, was intrigued by the EMF strength meter, so I let him handle that. Cameraman Tom was using the Hi8 camera with night vision, and Jim was recording on the regular, industrial-sized video camera. I used my Sony Mavica digital camera and RayTek thermal scanner. The other team members had their digital cameras, audio recorders, and camcorders.

We documented the lobby, which was once the living room when it was the innkeepers' residence. This is where Judge Wincklhofer conducted wedding ceremonies. While it was tastefully decorated for the Christmas holiday, nothing paranormal presented itself. We took our time photographing, filming, and measuring the temperature in all the first-floor dining rooms. When we were ready to head upstairs, we left an audio recorder in the dining room running to attempt to capture EVP while no one was around.

On the second floor were the former bedrooms, which are now dining rooms. They vary in size to accommodate two-person dinners and twenty-person dinner parties. The largest of these rooms is Miss Mack's. She was the last boarder to live at the Cranbury Inn and died in 1982 of old age. Gay was certain that Miss Mack's spirit still lingers at the inn. We took some ambient temperature readings of the room as well as photographs. The average air temperature was sixty-seven degrees, and we found no anomalies in the digital photos.

Gay suggested that she try to contact Miss Mack and have *Digithead* film the impromptu séance. Séances and spirit provocation are against NJGHS protocol, but it was up to the show's producer, not me. Jim agreed to film it. We all took our seats around the large dining table. I was at the corner of the table seated next to the gentleman from HBO. Gay began to speak, "Miss Mack, it's Gay. There are some people here who would like to meet you. Can you give us a sign that you're here?"

I pointed my thermal scanner at the duct on the wall and registered a temperature of 106.5 degrees. Gay explained it was so hot because it acted as an exhaust duct for the kitchen. We sat there quietly waiting for a sign from Miss Mack. I kept an eye on the thermal scanner and the temperature was hovering around the 106 degree mark. Suddenly, there was a slam. We all jumped in our seats, and the HBO man yelled, "What the hell was that?" Gay went to inspect the area the sound came from. "It's just this old window. Someone left it open and it fell closed," she said.

Everyone took a deep breath and regained composure, and Gay asked again for Miss Mack to visit with us. I saw my thermal scanner register a drop in temperature. It was just a few degrees, but as I began to announce this drop in temperature to the group, it picked up speed. It nose-dived to eighty-seven degrees in a matter of seconds. I knew something was present in front of the duct. I put down the thermal scanner and picked up the digital camera to take some pictures. I didn't capture the presence on camera. However, one of the other investigators took a picture of a small orb moving along the floor on his end of the dining room. He was seated approximately fifteen feet across from the duct.

We concluded the session and moved along to the other dining rooms. Chip noted an EMF reading of 0.2 milligauss in the dinner-for-two dining room, and an NJGHS member captured an orb here at the same time. I went down the hall to the ladies' room. Women have reported seeing a ghostly female in this room. In some instances, women have been washing their hands or doing their makeup and noticed a woman standing behind them in the reflection of the mirror. When they turn around to look directly at her, she is not there. Sometimes this ghost appears as a misty form by the stall door. I took pictures and waited patiently to see if she would show up. However, the guys were getting anxious about heading up to the attic, so I answered their calls and met them at the foot of the stairs that led to the attic.

The staircase was narrow, and the door to the attic was tiny. We had to crawl through this door and hoist ourselves up onto the beams and planks of plywood that passed for a floor. Once we had everyone positioned safely, I took the temperature reading. It was averaging between thirty-eight and forty-four degrees. The attic was quite dusty given the exposed insulation, but we did manage to capture some valid orb pictures. By following the NJGHS protocols, we took turns taking the pictures to avoid capturing someone's autofocus beam and took several pictures in succession in the same spot when we detected an orb. Dust particles show up on film as a swirling mass, but we were getting a few separate orbs in one picture followed by no orbs at all in the next. To further validate our findings, Tom's Hi8 camera captured the orbs in motion. We did not capture any EVP.

In the final production of the show, *Digithead* revealed the crew's untouched, unedited film footage of the attic orbs and orbs they captured coming down the second-floor hallway and disappearing into a wall. However, they did have to slow the footage down to frame-by-frame mode for the viewers to see, as orbs move at a lightning speed.

The show aired in January 2002 and was well received. Jim said it was one of their most viewed shows. I could tell people were watching it by the increase in hits on the NJGHS Web site and the e-mails I was receiving.

Were the orbs we captured those of slaves who were unable to escape to Canada on the Underground Railroad? Perhaps the orbs in the hallway were those of Miss Mack and William Christie, who died in front of the Cranbury Inn on October 14, 1796, after a fall from his stagecoach. He is buried across the street in the Presbyterian Church graveyard.

In 2004 I returned with a television crew from the network M6 in Paris. This time Gay told me that she didn't want to publicize the paranormal activity anymore because it had lost bookings for two wedding receptions. Apparently the brides-to-be were superstitious and canceled when they learned of the ghost stories associated with the inn. I assured Gay that this would only air in France. She agreed to let us film, and we captured some interesting photos once again in the attic. I never did get a copy of the piece as the M6 people had promised. Therefore, I have no idea whether they captured any paranormal anomalies on their high-end television equipment.

If you go to the Cranbury Inn yourself, be mindful of the diners who are less enthusiastic about ghosts. Book a private dining room on the second floor. Ladies, pack your digital camera in your dress purse and make frequent trips to the loo. There's nothing like a little undercover ghost hunting to boost the appetite.

Southern
New Jersey

OCEAN

BURLINGTON

CAMDEN

GLOUCESTER

ATLANTIC

CUMBERLAND

*ATLANTIC
OCEAN*

CAPE
MAY

**SOUTHERN
NEW JERSEY**

*DELAWARE
BAY*

Mount Holly
Burlington County Prison Museum

Cape May Court House
Cape May County Museum

CHAPTER 33

Burlington County Prison Museum

MOUNT HOLLY

THE BURLINGTON COUNTY PRISON MUSEUM makes for a nice family day trip. It is not nearly as imposing and threatening as the Eastern State Penitentiary in Philadelphia. The pretty, tree-lined streets and striking Victorian homes of quaint Mount Holly surround this prison.

I gave a presentation on ghost hunting in September 2007 at the Burlington County Library. Afterward, I was approached by a woman and her daughter. They wanted to know whether I had ever been to the prison. I told them I had not but would love to come back down and see it. The daughter was a volunteer for the haunted house the prison museum has during the Halloween season. She insisted I check out the prison as she had an overwhelming creepy feeling while working there to build the haunted house.

The prison was completed in 1811 to house forty inmates. It was designed by the architect Robert Mills. The prison's architectural design and sturdy concrete-and-brick construction resulted in a maintenance-free building with fireproofing, heating, and ventilation systems. The prison operated until 1965, its 154 years of service qualifying it as the oldest continually used prison in the United States. At the time of its closing, the prison was grossly overcrowded: approximately one hundred inmates were incarcerated.

On a clear, sunny Sunday afternoon in March 2008, I met Ron Reed, the docent on duty, at the prison. Ron is a very relaxed and down-to-earth man. He was helpful to me in pointing out the brochure and the timeline on the wall and later answering my questions about paranormal activity. Both Ron and Marisa Bozarth, another volunteer, appeared on the Sci Fi Channel's show *Ghost Hunters* when the Atlantic Paranormal Society (TAPS) visited the prison at the behest of Dave Tango's father.

I began my self-guided tour in the warden's office. I had my Nikon Coolpix in one hand and my Sony digital audio recorder in the other. I wandered up the stairs in the women's section. I took pictures and didn't see anything beyond what I was taking a picture of. For some reason, I usually have good luck at getting orb shots on stairwells.

I walked into the first hallway on my right with a couple cells that had no doors on them. I walked right into these cells hoping to feel the sense of not being alone or to capture a former inmate's voice on my recorder. I didn't have any odd sensations while standing alone in the first cell, nor in the second one. I took some pictures, but nothing out of the ordinary appeared. I went back out into the main hallway and headed toward the stairs while stopping to dictate the signs I was reading into my audio recorder. I read how there were seven hangings at the prison from 1807 to 1906. The last hanging, on March 24, 1906, was for Rufus Johnson and George Small, who were convicted for the murder of English-born governess Florence Allinson of Moorestown. I continued along my tour to the "dungeon," the maximum-security cell. The most hardened criminals were held here, usually awaiting their hanging, but there were only seven hangings in one hundred years. When I hear the word "dungeon," I picture a dark, dank room in a basement. This cell, however, is on the top floor of the prison to prevent the convict from digging his way to freedom. His ability to communicate with other prisoners was limited as well because the cell is inside areas where the guards patrolled and has only one small window up high. Unlike the other cells, the dungeon has

Sculptures of prisoners

no fireplace. In the picture I took of this cell, there is a sculpture of a prisoner chained to the center of the floor. That was the custom then. Unlike the prisoner sculpture, inmates in the dungeon at that time would have been stripped naked. Obviously, with little children passing through this museum's halls and cells, it was a better model to have a fully clothed figure chained to the floor.

Joel Clough was a murderer who spent his last night in the dungeon before his hanging. In the Burlington County Prison episode of *Ghost Hunters*, I heard Marisa Bozarth say that in this cell, visitors will smell cigarette smoke. She also said that Joel's body was buried in an unmarked grave in the prison yard as he had no family and no church cemetery wanted a murderer buried in their sacred ground. Shortly after Joel's execution, Marisa said, prison guards would smell cigarette smoke in the dungeon, and other prisoners feared the cell because of the anguished moans and groans that came from it. Most people believe that the odor and the sounds come from the ghost of Joel Clough.

The dungeon door was closed and locked, so I couldn't tour it. I did manage to take a picture by positioning my camera in between the iron bars of the door. I didn't capture any anomaly in this photo, and I did not smell or hear any otherworldly scents or sounds while standing there quietly for a few moments after taking the picture.

I continued down the hall to a bridge hallway connecting the warden's home to the prison. As I entered this connecting hallway, I looked out the window at the prison yard and directly down on the gallows—a replica, not what was actually used in hangings that took place here. I continued on to the warden's home. The two little rooms I could enter here were outfitted with displays of items retrieved from the property over the years. There were some old handcuffs, homemade tools and "shivs" (makeshift weapons). I couldn't resist taking a photo of the hanging

caption?

hood that was secured over a Styrofoam head by a rope.

I left this room to head back down the connecting hallway to the prison. As I reached the landing at the end of the connection, I took some pictures of the stairs. Suddenly, I could smell cigarette smoke. I quickly turned on my digital audio recorder and said, “If there is someone here and you could tell me your name, that would be great.” I didn’t bother to stop and check the recorder at that moment. I let it run. When I got home, I listened to my recordings. I got a response! I’m not completely sure what the entire message is, but it sounds like a young man’s voice answering me. The one word that is clear is “crimes,” and after he says this, there is the sound of an exhaled puff. I just knew something was there with me when I started smelling cigarette smoke. The odor left, completely. I went all the way down the stairs to the basement hoping to find a plausible explanation.

No one was on the stairs or the landings as I walked down. I found an open exit door to the prison courtyard, but it was too far from the stairs for someone to be outside having a cigarette and having its scent trail up to where I was. I should also note there were no windows open where I was standing and smelling the cigarette smoke.

While out in the courtyard, I decided to take some pictures of the gallows and the prison building. The ground was too soft to allow me to visit the corner of the yard where they supposedly buried Joel Clough. I went back inside to see if I could trace the cigarette smoke smell once more.

I was back up on that landing. I didn't smell any smoke or scent other than the mustiness of a 197-year-old building. I waited and took some more pictures while letting my digital audio recorder run. Upon review of this last recording, I didn't hear any EVP.

I went back down to the lobby entrance and spoke with Ron, the docent. I remembered his telling me when I arrived that he has "an understanding" with the ghosts of the prison. He said, "They can't bother me or take my cigarettes, and I promise not to bring in a priest and exorcise them out of here." I asked him whether he had had a cigarette while I was upstairs touring the place. He assured me that he had not been smoking and that no one was allowed to smoke inside the museum. Later on, when I was taking pictures outside of the warden's house, I noticed a sign on the front window that reads, "No Smoking within 25 Feet of Building Entrances."

I told Ron about what I smelled upstairs on the landing by the connecting hallway. He said that when the Atlantic Paranormal Society came to investigate, they experienced the cigarette smoke in the women's wing of the prison. In that episode, Jason and Grant followed the smoke smell through the women's wing and traced it to rising above their heads. They confirmed that the air outside was clear and fresh and therefore no one was smoking outside making the scent waft into the prison.

I'm glad I had the chance to speak with Ron. He went on to tell me about the time he was working with Marisa in the basement and she saw a shadow walk by at the end of the hall. Ron didn't see anything. He said he simply suggested finishing up what they were doing and making a hasty exit. He felt uncomfortable and just wanted to get out of there as fast as possible.

Ron has conducted his own investigations by leaving his analog audio recorder in various parts of the prison to record EVP. He even captured an EVP that he played for me. He said that he and Marisa were the only ones in the building and were talking about someone when Ron remembered he had left the recorder going. He motioned to Marisa to be silent so he could retrieve the recorder and turn it off, and then they could continue their conversation. Later on, he rewound the tape and listened to it. He could hear someone saying the word "hanging." I put on his headphones, and he told me to listen after the clicking noise for the word. Sure enough, I heard it. The voice is not Marisa's. It sounds male, but it's definitely not Ron's—it had a much higher pitch than Ron's.

I was excited about my visit to this prison. I couldn't wait to get home and listen to my recordings and review my photographs. While driving home, I called my friend and NJGHS's technical advisor, Brian Sandt. I got his voice mail and left him a message about how thrilled I was at the experience of smelling the cigarette smoke on that landing. I just knew I had to have captured something. The pictures came out well for regular photos but were disappointing on a paranormal level. The first five audio recordings I listened to were ordinary: nothing beyond the sound of my voice reading the various signs on my self-guided tour. The sixth recording was the one where I smelled the cigarette and asked whether someone was there and to tell me their name. I have posted this EVP on the NJGHS Web site's The Deadline page (http://njghs.net/thedeadline.html) for people to listen to and send me their thoughts on its message. Like I said, I can hear the word "crimes" and the puff exhale quite clearly.

On the TV show *Ghost Hunters*, the researchers concluded that the prison was the scene of a residual haunting and was not actively haunted. I disagree. A residual haunting is like a video- or audiotape on an endless loop. It replays itself over and over. Sometimes it plays at the same time every day or night, and sometimes it plays on the anniversary of the event it represents. Given the fact that the smoke smell traveled beyond the women's wing where the Atlantic Paranormal Society smelled it and that a voice can be heard in response to my query, I think the haunting displays a level of consciousness. Residuals have no conscious interaction with the living, and they remain in a set location repeating their action.

The prison is a popular place for paranormal investigators, but you don't need to be a member of an investigative team to visit the prison. I encourage you to make the trip to the Burlington County Prison Museum, and don't forget your camera and audio recorder.

CHAPTER 34

The Cape May County
Historical Museum
CAPE MAY COURTHOUSE

THE PROPERTY ON WHICH THE MUSEUM STANDS
was first purchased by Arthur Cresse in 1695. His grandson,
Robert Cresse, built a two-story house in 1755. Eventually this
structure was torn down, and in 1830 Robert Morris Holmes
built a new house, today a museum on the opposite side of the
highway from the original structure. Holmes died in 1840 without a will, and the property was divided among his three sons.
One son, Richard, bought out the other two brothers' shares
and named his farm Strabane in honor of the town his grandfather had come from in Ireland.

The house and property left the Holmes family after 150

years in 1935, when Richard's daughter, Emma, died. Judge Palmer Way then bought the property and used it as a summer vacation home with his family for twenty-two years. Dr. Ulric Lacquer and his wife, Christine, owned the property from 1957 to 1976. During that time, they moved an eighteenth-century barn onto the property as an art studio for Christine. They also added a greenhouse and a garage. In 1976 the Cape May County Historical and Genealogical Society acquired the property and turned it in to the lovely museum that is there today, complete with period rooms.

I was scheduled to present a talk on ghost hunting at the museum on Friday, October 19, 2007. Making the three-hour trip wasn't enough. Nooo, it had to be raining too. This slowed me down considerably. Where it wasn't raining, it was so foggy I couldn't see three feet past the headlights of my car. At one point I had quite a scare, and not of the paranormal kind. I almost drove off the road when the fog obscured a turn to the right and I headed straight.

My sons and I arrived a little late for my presentation. However, we got inside, set up the projector and computer in this little room, and were ready when the tour came in for my presentation.

After the presentation, I had the chance to talk with curator Pary Woehlcke, who booked me for the presentation. She has worked at the museum for several years and had some paranormal encounters. Pary is now in the habit of saying "hello" to the invisible residents each time she opens the museum for the day. She also announces why she is there and what she plans to do, whether it's work in the office or give historical tours. She says she feels this sets a more positive tone for the time she spends working in the museum.

Pary's most chilling encounter took place in the Old Toy Room, which was added around 1820, and, Pary claims, has a very strange feeling to it. One day, she was preparing some paperwork and needed the completion date for one of the needlepoint samplers. She went up to the Old Toy Room to examine the sampler and retrieve its date. While there, she put down her notepad and pen and picked up the sampler to examine it. In doing so, she bumped what she thought was a music box on the table, and a little song began to play. "Hmm, must be a music box," she said aloud. With that, the music stopped. She then said, "It was a pretty little song," and the music started to play again. She was so frightened that she put the sampler down, grabbed her pen and pad and said, "You can stay here and play," and left abruptly.

Later on that day, she went back up to the Old Toy Room with a museum volunteer, Matt Vendetta. Pary admitted to Matt that she was too unnerved to go back up there alone. Once they were in the room, they noticed a wind-up doll. Matt wound up the doll, but it made no sound. There was no music box in the room.

Matt is seventeen years old and started volunteering at the Cresse-Holmes House when he was thirteen as part of his Confraternity of Christian Doctrine project. After completing his project, he ended up accepting the offer to work part time giving tours and handling other tasks at the museum. He has had his share of otherworldly experiences working here.

Matt told me about the night he and another volunteer were sitting on the steps of the staircase that leads to the second floor. They both heard muffled voices coming from either the Doctor's Room, one of the period rooms, which displays period surgical instruments, or the living room. Matt and his colleague figured someone had remained behind after the last tour, so they went to see who was there. They thoroughly inspected both rooms and couldn't find anyone.

He told me about the time he and two other volunteers were heading up the stairs to the attic, and all three of them heard the distinct sound of a young girl humming right behind them. They turned around to find no one there. Matt believes this may be the spirit of the young girl who fell down the main staircase and died many years ago.

In the summer of 2007, he arrived one day for work and upon entering the building sensed this overwhelming anger, as if whatever spirit was present did not want Matt there that day. He felt frightened enough to want to leave. He was scared out of his wits, and when he made it to the office where his boss was already working, she commented to him how pale he was.

Matt also told me about the mannequin in the Victorian Room whose right arm would normally be in an upright position. He found it pointing downward but figured it was loose and merely a case of gravity at work. When he moved the arm back where it belonged, he realized how difficult it was to get the arm to move in either direction. No one else who could have moved the arm was in the museum.

Another time, he noticed the light that sits on the little blue desk in the Country Room was unplugged. He plugged in the light but did not turn it on. He left the room and came back a few minutes later, and the light was on. No one else had been in there. He would have heard or seen them. Matt knew he was the only one up there. Or was he? This could be written off to a faulty light bulb or wiring in the plug of the lamp. If it had been unplugged and shining brightly, that would have been a remarkable paranormal display.

One day, in addition to hearing phantom footsteps, Matt heard the sound of a door slamming while he was cleaning the Victorian Room. He figured somebody had closed the door to the Country Room, but when he checked, the doors to all the rooms were open.

Finally, Matt told me of the day he was sitting in Pary's office on the second floor with his back to the door. He was talking with Gabby, a museum intern. Mid-conversation he heard the sound of a little girl's giggle. He turned around quickly in the chair to see who it was. He didn't see anyone standing there. However, he did catch a glimpse of an amorphous shadow making its way across the wall.

I admit I did not come in contact with any ghosts while at the museum the night of my presentation. However, I could sense the feeling of not being completely alone while in the bathroom, a most unsettling feeling to be sure. I would suggest a trip to this museum. At the very least, you can enjoy touring the period rooms and learning about maritime history. As for the ghosts, they may tag along with you on a tour.

Ghosthunting
Travel Guide

AMERICA'S
HAUNTED ROAD TRIP

Visiting Haunted Sites

* **Acorn Hall** (973) 267-3465
68 Morris Ave., Morristown, NJ 07960-4212
http://www.acornhall.org

  Admission fees: adults, $6; seniors, $5; students, $3; children under 12, free

* **Baptist Church Cemetery** (908) 322-5487
333 Park Ave., Scotch Plains, NJ 07076

* **Bell's Mansion Restaurant** (973) 426-9977
11 Main St., Stanhope, NJ 07874
http://www.restaurantpassion.com/listing.aspx?a=561&sid=8&sn=NJ

* **Bernardsville Library (original structure)** (908) 766-0118
Two Morristown Rd., Bernardsville, NJ 07924
http://www.bernardsvillelibrary.org

* **Branch Brook Park** (973) 268-2300
Branch Brook Park Alliance, 115 Clifton Ave., Newark, NJ 07104
http://www.branchbrookpark.org

* **Burlington County Prison Museum** (609) 265-5476 or (609) 265-5858
128 High St., Mount Holly, NJ 08060
http://www.prisonmuseum.net

  Hours: Thursday–Saturday, 10 a.m.–4 p.m., Sunday, noon–4 p.m.
  Admission fees: adults, $4; students & seniors (55+), $2; children under 5, free

* **Cape May County Historical Museum** (609) 465-3535
The Cresse-Holmes House, 504 Route 9 North
Cape May Court House, NJ 08210
http://www.cmcmuseum.org

* **Centenary College** (908) 852-1400
400 Jefferson St., Hackettstown, NJ 07840
http://www.centenarycollege.edu

‣ **Charlie Brown's Steakhouse** (908) 979-0446
109 Grand Ave., Hackettstown, NJ 07840

‣ **Cranbury Inn** (609) 655-5595
21 South Main St., Cranbury, NJ 08512
http://www.thecranburyinn.com/

‣ **Drew University** (973) 408-3000
36 Madison Ave., Madison, NJ 07940
http://www.drew.edu

‣ **Excalibur** (312) 266-1944
632 North Dearborn Street, Chicago, IL 60610

Originally built in 1892 as the home of the Chicago Historical Society, the Romanesque-style brick building now houses Excalibur, a popular nightclub. If you can see through your dance partner, you know you've met one of Excalibur's resident ghosts.

‣ **Fox and Hound Tavern at the Lebanon Hotel** (908) 437-1300
69 Main St., Lebanon, NJ 08833
http://www.foxandhoundtavern.com/home.htm

Dinner reservations strongly recommended on weekends

‣ **Galloping Hill Golf Course** (908) 686-1556
21 N. 31st St., Kenilworth, NJ 07033
http://www.ucnj.org/parks/golf.html

‣ **Garden State Parkway**
Site of Christmas Eve 1998 bus crash
Rest stop between exits 123 and 124

‣ **Garret Mountain Reservation** (973) 881-4832
Passaic County Parks Department
311 Pennsylvania Ave., Paterson, NJ 07503
http://www.passaiccountynj.org/ParksHistorical/Parks/
garretmountainreservation.htm

✤ **Harry's Road House (now Synaxis at the Shore)**
662 Cookman Ave., Asbury Park, NJ 07712
http://www.asburymurder.com (Peter Lucia's e-book)

✤ **The Hermitage** (201) 445-8311
335 North Franklin Turnpike, Ho-Ho-Kus, NJ 07423
http://www.thehermitage.org

✤ **Hobart Manor at William Paterson University** (877) 978-3923
300 Pompton Rd., Wayne, NJ 07470
http://www.wpunj.edu/default.htm

✤ **Hotel Belvidere** (908) 475-2006
430 Front St., Belvidere, NJ 07823
http://www.hotelbelvidere.com

✤ **Lambert Castle Museum** (973) 247-0085
3 Valley Rd., Paterson, NJ 07503
http://www.lambertcastle.org

Admission fees: adults, $5; seniors (65+), $4; children ages 5–17, $3;
children under age 5, free. Children must be accompanied by an adult.

✤ **Laurel Grove Cemetery (Annie's Road)** (973) 956-0711
295 Totowa Rd., Totowa, NJ 07512

✤ **Liquid Assets Gentlemen's Club** (908) 753-0290 or (908) 812-2707
118 New Market Ave., South Plainfield, NJ 07080
http://www.liquidassetsnj.com/ghost.html

✤ **Macculloch Hall Historical Museum** (973) 538-2404
45 Macculloch Ave., Morristown, NJ 07960
http://www.maccullochhall.org

Open Sunday, Wednesday, Thursday: 1–4 p.m.

✤ **Pattenburg House** (908) 735-2547
512 County Road 614, Pattenburg, NJ 08802
http://www.myspace.com/pattenburghouse

❧ **Proprietary House** (732) 826-5527
149 Kearny Ave., Perth Amboy, NJ 08861
http://www.proprietaryhouse.org/home.html

❧ **The Publick House** (908) 879-6878
111 Main St., Chester, NJ 07930
http://www.chestertownship.org/history.html

❧ **The Raritan Public Library** (908) 725-0413
54 E. Somerset St., Raritan, NJ 08869
http://www.raritanlibrary.org

Open Monday through Saturday, but closed on Saturdays in July & August.

❧ **Ringwood Manor** (973) 962-2240
Sloatsburg Rd., Ringwood, NJ 07456
http://www.ringwoodmanor.com

❧ **Shades of Death Road and Ghost Lake**
Off of County Route 611 (Hope Road)
Great Meadows, NJ

❧ **The Spy House (Seabrook-Wilson House)**
719 Port Monmouth Rd., Port Monmouth, NJ
http://www.monmouthcountyparks.com/parks/bayshore.asp

❧ **The Stanhope House**
45 Main St., Stanhope, NJ 07874
http://www.stanhopehouse.com

Note: The Stanhope House is temporarily closed.

❧ **Summerhill Park (Ghost of Rose City)**
Ridgedale Ave., Madison, NJ 07940
http://www.rosenet.org

❧ **Surprise Lake, Watchung Reservation**
Off of Glenside Avenue, Summit, NJ
http://www.ucnj.org/parks/wrmap804.pdf (map)

≫ **Washington Cemetery** (908) 689-5818
203 S. Lincoln Ave., Washington, NJ 07882

≫ **The Washington Theatre** (908) 689-0899
165 E. Washington Ave. (Route 57), Washington, NJ 07882

≫ **Watchung Tower (Suicide Tower), Watchung Reservation**
Summit, NJ
http://www.ucnj.org/parks/wrmap804.pdf (map)

≫ **Westfield Presbyterian Church (Ghost of Baltus Roll)** (908) 233-0301
140 Mountain Ave., Westfield, NJ 07090
http://www.westfieldpc.org

≫ **The Whistling Swan Inn** (973) 347-6369
110 Main St., Stanhope, NJ 07874
http://www.whistlingswaninn.com

≫ **Yellow Frame Presbyterian Church** (973) 383-5364
One Yellow Frame Rd., Newton, NJ 07860
http://www.yellowframe.org

Ghostly Resources

Chapter 1

Madison Fire Department, "Mead Hall," http://www.rosenet.org/gov/fire/ communications.htm. Drew University, campus map, http://www.drew.edu/map/index.php?building=mead.

Chapter 2

Macken, Lynda Lee. *Ghosts of the Garden State*. pp. 21–22. Forked River, NJ; Black Cat Press, 2001.

Sceurman, Mark, and Mark Moran. *Weird N.J.: Your Travel Guide to New Jersey's Local Legends and Best Kept Secrets*. pp. 216–219. New York, NY; Barnes & Noble, 2003.

Chapter 3

Capone, Sally. "Book Recalls Murder That Rocked Madison", *Madison Eagle*, January 29, 2004.

No Author's Byline. "Brutal Murder of Twelve Year Old Girl Last Night," *Madison Eagle*, October 7, 1921.

No Author's Byline. "Detectives Seek Evidence Leading to Child's Slayer," *Madison Eagle*, October 14, 1921.

Chapter 4

Macken, Lynda Lee. *Ghosts of the Garden State Vol 2*. pp. 43–44. Forked River, NJ; Black Cat Press, 2003.

Riv, Paul. "Elvis Is Alive and Well at Garrett Mountain," *Weird N.J.*, no. 29: 57.

Peacock, Elaine, "The Madman of Garrett Mountain," *Weird N.J.*, no. 6: 13.

Chapter 9

Harpster, Richard E. "I Remember", *Hackettstown Weekly*, March 1996.

Nunn, J. Harold. *The People of Hackettstown*. p. 72.

Chapter 11

Hauck, Dennis William. *Haunted Places: The National Directory*. p. 279. New York, NY, Penguin Books, 1994, 1996, 2002.

Johnsonburg Christian Cemetery. "Read Family Connections," http://www.charm.net/~edrtjd/readgen/johnsch.htm.

Macken, Lynda Lee. *Ghosts of the Garden State Vol. 2.* pp. 19–20. Forked River, NJ, Black Cat Press, 2003.

No Author's Byline. "The Haunted Yellow Frame Church" *Weird N.J.*, no. 9: 35.

Yellow Frame Presbyterian Church, "Our History," http://www.yellowframe.org/Hist2.html.

Chapter 12

Meeker, Sharon, and Robert Meeker. *The Changewater Murders: A True Historical Account.* pp. 25–62. Budd Lake, NJ; Legacy of America, 1998.

Meeker, Sharon, and Robert Meeker. "Introduction and Companion to the Protest of Peter W. Parke Who Was Executed Friday, August 22, 1845 for The Changewater Murders." p. 6. Budd Lake, NJ; Legacy of America, 1998.

Washington Township. "Important Dates," http://www.washington-twp-warren.org/Government/General_Information/History___Tour/Important_dates/important_dates.html.

Chapter 14

The Hermitage. http://www.thehermitage.org.

Macken, Lynda Lee. *Ghosts of the Garden State Vol. 3.* pp. 31–33. Forked River, NJ; Black Cat Press, 2005.

Chapter 15

Historic Hacksettstown (Hackettstown Historical Society). "The Mystery of Tillie Smith," www.hackettstownhistory.com/narticle_tilliesmith.shtml.

Macken, Lynda Lee. *Ghosts of the Garden State Vol. 2.* pp. 23–25. Forked River, NJ; Black Cat Press, 2003.

Chapter 16

Macken, Lynda Lee. *Ghosts of the Garden State Vol. 2.* pp. 13–14. Forked River, NJ; Black Cat Press, 2003

Chapter 17

Macken, Lynda Lee. *Ghosts of the Garden State*. pp. 10–11. Forked River, NJ; Black Cat Press, 2001

Moss, Laura; Baker, John J.; Rosser, Cathleen. "Three Ghostly Legends of Hobart Manor at William Paterson College," *Weird N.J.*, no. 13: 62.

Ross, Terry E., William Paterson University, "Ghosts, Legends, and Other Strange Happenings . . . ," http://ww2.wpunj.edu/aboutus/Hobart/Hobartmanor_tr.htm.

The Pioneer-Times, "Weird William Paterson" (a history of Hobart Manor), http://www.pioneertimeswpu.com/media/paper756/news/2005/05/17/CampusNews/Weird.William.Paterson-951042.shtml.

Chapter 19

Cool, Kevin, "New Age Thinking," *Stanford Magazine*. http://www.stanfordalumni.org/news/magazine/2004/julaug/features/aging.html#topofpage.

Hauck, Dennis William. *Haunted Places: The National Directory*. p. 273. New York, NY, Penguin Books, 1994, 1996, 2002.

Klein, Bruce J., "The Wonderful Lengthening of Lifespan," The Longevity Meme. http://www.longevitymeme.org/articles/viewarticle.cfm?article_id=11.

Macken, Lynda Lee. *Ghosts of the Garden State*. pp. 19–20. Forked River, NJ; Black Cat Press, 2001.

Spectral Review. "Bernardsville Library Investigated" (John Maddaluna's account of witnessing Phyllis Parker in the 1950s), http://www.spectralreview.com/2008/01/13/bernardsville-library-investigated/.

Chapter 20

Lebanon Fire Company. "The History of the Lebanon Fire Company," http://www.18fire.org/history.php.

Macken, Lynda Lee. *Ghosts of the Garden State Vol. 2*, pp. 30–31. Forked River, NJ; Black Cat Press, 2003.

Chapter 22

No Author's Byline. "Woman's Body Found on Railroad Track," *New York Times*, Dec. 20, 1902.

Ross, Jason, "13 Bumps Road Revisited," *Weird N.J.*, no. 13: 49.

Township of Scotch Plains. "History," http://www.scotchplainsnj.com/history_main.html.

Chapter 23

No Author's Byline. A list of the obits: *New York Times*, obituaries, April 30, 1916.

No Author's Byline. "Fatal Blast in Jersey Mountain Rail Tunnel; Eight Injured Men Heroically Rescued," *New York Times*, Oct. 30, 1927.

No Author's Byline. "The Pattenburg Riots—Trial of John Bogue," *New York Times*, May 3, 1873.

No Author's Byline. "The Pattenburg Riot—Trial of David College for the Murder of the Negro Dennis Powell," *New York Times*, April 29, 1873.

Chapter 24

Barrett, Eleanor. "Ghost Breezes by to Thrill Chill Seekers," *Newark Star-Ledger*, Jan. 31, 1996.

No Author's Byline. "Real Story of 'Haunted' Raritan Library Is Ghastly, Not Ghostly Horrors Lurking in the Books, Not the Shelves," *Newark Star-Ledger*, Feb. 1, 1996.

No Author's Byline. "Parapsychologists Team Checks Out Library Ghost," *Newark Star-Ledger*, Jan. 31, 1996.

Chapter 25

No Author's Byline. "How Suicide Tower Got Its Name," *Weird N.J.*, no. 17: 38–39.

No Author's Byline. "Town Mourns Deaths of 3 Youths Killed in Crash," *Chatham Courier*, Aug. 16, 1984.

Chapter 28

"Driver Questioned in Deadly New Jersey Bus Crash," CNN.com, http://www.cnn.com/US/9812/25/nj.bus.accident/index.html.

"8 Die When Bus Flips Over on Garden State Parkway," CNN.com, http://www.cnn.com/US/9812/24/nj.bus.accident.03/.

Chapter 29

Baltusrol Golf Club. "Club History at Baltusrol Golf Club,"
http://www.baltusrol.org/club/scripts/section/section.asp?NS=PCH.

The Roll Family Genealogy. "The Roll Family Windmill,"
http://homepages.rootsweb.com/~windmill/html/baltusro.html.

Chapter 30

Proprietary House. "History," http://www.proprietaryhouse.org/history.html.

ACKNOWLEDGMENTS

I WOULD LIKE TO THANK JEFF BELANGER, who recommended me for this project. Having worked with Jeff in the past, I realize what a high compliment this is. I would like to thank John Kachuba for his support and critique throughout the "birthing process" of this book. Thanks to Rosemary Ellen Guiley, Ph.D., for her support and endorsement of the project: "You should write this book. Why let someone else get all the glory?" Many thanks go to Jane Doherty. Jane and I go way back, and some of the best experiences I've had in the paranormal field are truly thanks to her.

Thanks to all the inn and restaurant owners who took time out of their hectic schedules to sit and interview with me.

I appreciate my team leaders of the New Jersey Ghost Hunters Society: Brian Sandt, Gregory and Sherry Irish, Laura Lindemann, and Dina Chirico. They are not only the most dedicated ghost hunters I know; they are my most trusted confidants in the operation and maintenance of this large paranormal investigating organization.

Of course, I have to thank my family, who have endured my fascination with ghosts and the paranormal, and who now will have to explain the silent *H* to more people who pick up this book and try to read my surname aloud. My sons, Brian and Trent, have been my biggest source of inspiration for this book. They reflect back to me my wonder and awe of this incredible field of study, and that has recharged my "writer's batteries" endlessly. Special thanks to my dad, who introduced me to *The Twilight Zone* and challenged me as a writer throughout my academic career. Mom, thanks for taking me to work with you on those school holidays at the Wedgewood Inn. Little did I know then that the very fear of seeing the ghost of Phoebe in the mirror of that private dining room would be my life's pursuit and passion.

About the Author

L'Aura Hladik's interest in the paranormal started in childhood and culminated with living in an actual haunted rental house when she was in the eighth grade. In 1993 she officially began hunting for ghosts, and in 1998 she founded the New Jersey Ghost Hunters Society, which is the largest organization of its kind in the "Garden State." (www.njghs.net)

In addition to ghost hunting, writing about ghosts, and presenting her findings to schools and libraries over the years, she's also appeared on the nationally syndicated talk show "Montel Williams" as well as local cable shows and New Jersey's own radio station, 101.5 FM.

L'Aura's ghost research takes her beyond the borders of New Jersey to other states—even other countries, such as Ireland. Yet, the "Jersey Girl" always comes home to her favorite haunt. One of L'Aura's most prized possessions is her 1983 Cadillac Fleetwood, affectionately known as Jezzabelle.